THE LITTLE BOOK OF BROKEN CAR THOUGHTS

BY: TOM SANTOSPAGO

authorHOUSE®

AuthorHouse™
1663 Liberty Drive
Bloomington, IN 47403
www.authorhouse.com
Phone: 1 (800) 839-8640

Published by AuthorHouse 06/19/2015

ISBN: 978-1-5049-1850-3 (sc)
ISBN: 978-1-5049-1849-7 (e)

Library of Congress Control Number: 2015909881

Print information available on the last page.

CONTENTS

For every entrepreneur behind the wheel
in family-owned dealerships

ABOUT THE AUTHOR

Tom Santospago, CEO of Dealership-180, has worked in car and truck dealerships for more than thirty years. He learned the business from the bottom up, gaining a comprehensive understanding of how to ensure that each department within a dealership functions at peak performance to maximize profits. In his position as CEO of Dealership-180, Tom leads a motivated team dedicated to turning dealerships 180 degrees away from underperformance to put them on the road to profitability. He has successfully implemented the three-car system in stores selling Mercedes-Benz, Ferrari, Toyota, Ford, Nissan, VW, Hyundai, Acura, Lincoln, Mercury, and Chevrolet. To learn more, check out Tom's website (www.dealership-180.com).

INTRODUCTION

When I'm called into a dealership that is underperforming due to either a lack in sales volume or low overall dealership gross, I find that the reasons all have a common thread. Usually, it's not because of the car line they sell, the location they're in, their employees, or even the advertising. In fact, there's only one main reason why a dealership isn't maximizing profits—fear. Yes, it's that simple. Fear. The entrepreneur behind the wheel isn't willing to take the necessary risks to change the status quo in favor of enhanced profitability, even if those changes promise a brighter future for everyone involved in the business.

Ask yourself a few questions. If your store is not performing, do you know why? Have you really taken a good look at your company to identify its strengths and weaknesses? One department may be pulling another down, or more likely, all the departments in the dealership are out of sync and failing to maximize profits through improved efficiency and customer service.

If you already know this is the case, why haven't you made important changes? Do you fear losing employees? Do you fear rocking the boat, upsetting the applecart, throwing mud in the water? Well, change is the only constant in life, and it most assuredly is the only constant in business, regardless of whether the change is positive or negative.

So, you have a choice. Stick with what you've always done and operate below your potential, or carefully analyze your business and reach for the stars—because the sky really is the limit! You just have to believe in yourself and in the people you choose to have on your team.

A dealer from a premium franchise recently admitted to me that he avoids changes to keep his staff intact. His employees are nice, hardworking individuals, but they're stuck in a rut. They've been with him for twenty years, and he can't imagine the company without them.

So, is he right to maintain the status quo even though he knows there's something wrong, even though he knows he should probably move people to different positions or even let them go? Inertia is a recipe for disaster. It can lead to bankruptcy, but more likely it will result in stagnation that blocks all roads to a better tomorrow.

But there is a better way to help your management team succeed. A better way for that team to help your salespeople! And a better way for the team to help your salespeople help your customers.

That better way stems from an understanding of how crucial alignment among all of your departments is for success. The proper alignment of your departments will change the entire working environment for the customers, employees, management team, and ownership.

I designed my company, Dealership-180, to help the small family dealership contend in today's competitive marketplace, and I created it because I want to arm family-owned dealerships with a real sales process to set them apart from competition.

I see so many sales processes that look great on paper but fall apart in real-life sales experience. The processes you find in this book will not only give your sales team complete alignment, they will give your customers the sales experience they dream of. I always look at a company like a three-legged stool: one leg is customer satisfaction, one leg is employee satisfaction, and the third is profitability. Pull one leg off, and the stool tips over!

At Dealership-180, we take small family dealerships and turn them around 180 degrees toward volume, growth, and profitability. I can walk into any underperforming dealership and outline everything that needs to be done in order to turn the ship around 180 degrees, just like it was in plain sight for everyone to see. I can look into an employee's eyes and read that person like an old high-school textbook, as well as motivate and lead him or her to the top of the game. I have a knack for finding ways to get customers through the door, and to provide service, parts, and most of all, sales. All of this I can do while building a real brand that sets the dealership apart from the big boys.

In turning dealerships around, there are many elements that have to be in place, but there are three that stand above the rest. The first one is the "three-car system," which separates you and your sales team from all the other dealerships in your market. The second element is "selling with indifference," which separates your salespeople, management team, and service team from all other dealerships. The third element is the "alignment of all dealership departments." Aligning your team not only yields satisfaction for you, the dealer, your employees, and your customers but also brings major net to your dealership every month.

Let's face it; it is no secret that happy dealership employees give you happy customers. And it's no secret that those two things combined together, tied in with the multicar system in team alignment, will bring you to places you never thought were possible before.

I'll go into much more detail in the following pages, but let's first take a quick look at what I call the three-car system, which is a selling system that allows the customer to shop and compare vehicles by comparing prices, retail payment, and leases. Instead of shopping around at multiple dealerships with multiple salespeople, it allows customers to do it under one roof.

The process starts off on the right foot by getting a better understanding of the customer's needs, budget, and must-haves. It allows the salesperson to show multiple scenarios to the customer while educating him or her on market-based pricing. Think of it this way: When you walk in to purchase a cellular phone, is there only one plan to choose from? Do they negotiate on price or do you pick the plan that's right for you? Along with a nonconfrontational style, both allow for a natural buying process for the customer and salesperson.

In the following pages, I will give you your road map for change. I truly believe the following: Once you embrace change, you can begin moving forward, and you will have the ability to see things from an entirely new perspective. Some dealers I've worked with have said, "It feels like a whole new dealership." The new atmosphere was achieved with most of the same people, budget, and inventory.

Some dealers have also said, "The solutions were in front of me the whole time, and I never saw them." I always remind the person that it often takes an objective viewpoint to see the trees through the forest. If you're stuck in the rut of underperformance, your first step is recognizing it and accepting that there's a need to shake things up a bit to move forward. And that means not being afraid. The next step is simply going from passive to active mode when it comes down to running your car or truck dealership with the pedal to the metal!

So, it's time to hit the road! There's a big, wide world of success waiting just over the horizon! Let's go for it!

CHAPTER 1

BROKEN THOUGHTS

Part of my job as a consultant charged with turning dealerships around involves some detective work. I go through the entire business with a fine-tooth comb to see how every department functions. I look at how the employees interact with management, and how all the employees interact with customers. This process of analysis inevitably turns up what I define as "broken thoughts." Essentially, broken thoughts are excuses management makes for not moving forward or for not making the changes that are needed—all because of the fear of change.

But what the owner and managers forget is that the fear should be centered on what happens if things continue the way they are. When broken thought is eliminated, there is no limit for growth! When I begin pointing out the broken thoughts that permeate a company, the dealers start giving me reasons why they have kept the same people year after year even though the number in fixed sales continues to drop. The dealer starts the conversation with how loyal the team has been to the dealership, so the dealer has been loyal to them regardless of the performance and end results. So I always ask the dealer the same question: Why do you think your management team has become so ineffective over time?

Look out; here come the broken thoughts. Let me give you the top five broken thoughts about why you and your management team cannot be as successful as the same-brand dealerships in your marketplace.

1. We almost never make a change in the staff due to low performance; we usually do it for other reasons.
2. My management team has tried that before, and it just doesn't work at this store.
3. The general manager would like to change things, but he can't get the buy-in from his management team.
4. The management team feels they would lose key staff members if they had to dramatically change the way they have been doing things.
5. My management team may not be aggressive, but they always show up to work on time, and I'm sure they would never steal from me.

These are all reasons that prevent dealerships from moving forward, but I would like you to take a different approach to this. Assuming you have separate managers for each department, have them list the top five functions they do as managers that make them extremely successful. Also have each of them list all the day-to-day activity, breaking down what makes each of them successful at managing their teams.

This is where you can label the type of managers you have. It's important how each manager lists his or her duty and what's most important to them. What a manager was hired for and what he actually does could be two different things. Here is a classic example.

A Dealer Scenario

A dealership in the state of Maine had a sales manager who worked deals on the desk and managed six salespeople. The owner of the store decided to get him some help on the desk and hired him a floor manager. The owner's thought was that this newly hired manager could get involved when it came time to close a deal. The owner also thought that he could help follow up on all the deals with the salespeople each day. Some other tasks the owner had for him included following up with each new delivery so they could improve their customer satisfaction. Also, this new sales manager would get involved with training the salespeople.

Sounds like a good idea, right? The new manager at this point had been at the dealership for over two years and was handling these tasks he had been hired for—or so the owner thought! When I had that manager list his day-to-day activity, the list was a lot different than what he was hired for.

The first thing on his list was to make a fresh pot of coffee (I kid you not!). The next was to make sure everyone on the sales team clocked in. Then he had the stocking of new and used cars. The next item on this list was writing the used-car keeper checks. The list went on and on, but guess what wasn't on his list? Closing deals, training the salespeople, customer follow-up, and daily sales meetings. This new manager filled his day with administrative duties.

This gets even better. The sales manager, whose title was general sales manager, had the new manager closing the store most nights so he could leave early. Instead of having one manager penciling deals and the other manager working with the salespeople and customers, one manager was tied to the sales desk without the ability to move around the showroom and talk to customers while helping the sales staff make deals. In addition, this new manager wasn't allowed to appraise trades, so if there was a trade, the customer was told to come back the next day.

This is why it's important to have a clear understanding of what to expect out of your staff, especially your management team. You don't want them to be operating with broken thoughts. It's just bad business.

Making No Excuses

Here's something I hear all the time: "If I make my sales staff sit every customer down and get some information before they head out to the lot and pick out a vehicle, my top earners will run screaming from the room. And if my top sales staff quits, I will never be able to replace them."

That sort of thinking is a prime example of broken thoughts. The broken thought actually has a couple of levels. The first is thinking that your staff would not follow a three-car system that requires a little more work but will also generate more cash for everyone in the company while beefing up customer satisfaction. The core premise behind the three-car system is based on the belief that the customer will tell us how to close the sale if we only listen and respond to what we hear. This takes time, and it takes effort as well. Some sales staff won't want to go with the flow, but the best of your people will see that a more customer-oriented approach is in everyone's best interest.

Bear in mind that resistance to change almost always stems from fear. If you are afraid that requiring your staff to learn and follow the three-car system will cause a stampede for the door, then you'll never take the action necessary to implement new ways of doing things that will grow the business.

Living in fear is actually harder than making the necessary changes to get you out of a broken-thought modality. You will find them in most departments. Don't be afraid to search for them. Flush them out of the weeds and get rid of them as soon as possible!

Let's take a quick look at some broken thoughts as they apply to your sales and service departments.

Sales Department

Have you ever made the following excuses for not making changes?

- We cannot compete with the megadealers.
- I cannot afford to pay good people to work here.
- We can never generate the floor traffic in this market to have any kind of volume.
- Customers pay cash in this dealership or use their own bank, so we can't make money in finance. Besides, our warranties cost too much, and the customers don't have the time to wait for a finance manager.
- Our salespeople like to close their own deals.

- Our customers don't want to see lease or finance figures; they just want the bottom line.
- The sales staff won't like doing it that way; we will lose them if we try to change the sales process.

The bottom line is that excuses are reasons for failure, not success. Making excuses for inaction plays into your fear of change.

Parts and Service Department

Do you readily accept broken thoughts when it comes to efficiency and profitability in your parts and service department? The following are some common examples of broken thoughts. Some may sound disturbingly familiar.

- The service manager has been here for years, and he cannot see us competing with the Quik Lube franchises. There's no way we can make any money competing with quick service at the price the franchise is able to charge.
- We don't have a true system for our service advisers, but we really don't need one; my guy knows what to do.
- We let our advisers make all of our service appointments; they know how to fill the schedule.
- We can't find good techs who want to work here unless we overpay them.
- We can't teach our own techs from scratch, and even if we did, someone else would steal them once they got good.

The list goes on and on with all these excuses and misconceptions of why this "will never work." Ideally, you would simply realize that the fear of change is stopping you from the growth that the company so badly needs. You'd understand that some of your thoughts are broken. Does this sound familiar? Are you making excuses for failure?

Let's take the small dealership that has never done much volume as an example to make some key points.

A Dealer Scenario

The store owners made a moderate amount of money and watched every expense. No real decisions were made by anyone, including the owners who seemed to spend most of their time in front of an office computer. The dealership was eventually purchased, and I was given the task to run it for the new owners. Although this dealership was on a fairly busy road, the population of the town and surrounding area was much less in comparison to the large city dealers where I had worked before.

The story is almost always the same in every dealership in need of a 180-degree flip. Good people, good owners, and a parts and service business that's been plugging along for years. The thought process is also the same: "We are doing a great job for what's in our market."

But ask yourself if that's really true. It's easy to say everything is fine, because if we admit that there's room for improvement, it means we're not totally fine. It means we have work to do. It means we have to stop making excuses. At Dealership-180, we take the same team, move the right people around to best fit their skills, and we all agree on the plan moving forward.

The ones who embrace the new team plan quickly become a part of the strong results. The ones who live in fear of change go down two different paths. Some witness the entire staff do well and grow—so much so that they finally move over to the positive side. Others take the easy path. They say, "*I can't work here,* so I'm leaving." I wish that person luck and send him or her away.

Six months down the road, after the dealership is thriving under the auspices of the three-car system, some of the employees who left return to see if they can get their old jobs back. They tell me that they can't believe how successful we have become, almost as if it is the biggest surprise in the world.

In some cases, I do rehire them and find them to be some of my best employees and team players. In other cases, I don't rehire the employee. Negativity can do just as much harm as fear. It's always a judgment call, but it's one where a broken thought can create lasting negative impacts on the company.

After things turn around, I also get a kick out of the reaction of the store's previous owners. They inevitably speak with some of their old employees who had typically worked for them for twenty years. They ask how things are going, and when they find out how great things are, they get a little flustered, a little puzzled, and sometimes a little annoyed.

"How did you turn the dealership around so quickly?" they ask.

"How did you motivate Joe when I never could?"

I never would have guessed that! The former dealer's principals are like little children opening gifts at Christmas, only they can't keep it because it's not theirs to keep anymore. They can't believe that the bar was set; a plan was put into process; and surprise, it's a success! In some cases, we would sell more cars in three months than the previous dealer would have sold in a full year.

In one case that comes to mind, the dealer grossed about a $150,000 a month profit between new and used cars and the finance department. Three months later, we rose to $500,000, and a year later we were at $800,000 a month—not to even mention what happened in the parts and service department.

Working with What You Have

What do you really want to accomplish in your dealership? Ask yourself: Can I sell the volume I really want to? Do I have the right people? Can I get the right people? Can my building take the increase in volume? Will my people leave me if I change too much? Will customer satisfaction turn from green to red? Will I lose everything I worked for? These are some tough questions, but they must be asked and answered.

As I walk through a dealership, I make contact with each employee as he or she goes about his or her business. I make small talk with all employees, and I look at the way they handle customers and other employees. I ask them if I can have a few minutes later in the day to get their opinion on something. Hours after my walk through the dealership, the owner/general manager starts asking me questions about each employee.

Quite often the owners/general managers are very surprised on how I envision utilizing their current employees in new roles or ways within the dealership. Change doesn't mean blowing everything up and starting from scratch (or at least, usually it doesn't). Chances are you've got all you need.

It's just a matter of rethinking how you operate to create better efficiency that can lead to increased profitability.

After meeting with the employees, I often find they are the right employees but in the wrong departments or in the wrong positions. Let me clarify this with a few examples of the right employee in the wrong job. In one store, I had a finance manager who had a good understanding of his department, but his finance numbers and after sales were on the average side at best. In talking to him, I discovered that he had been a finance manager for about five years. He said he took the promotion from the sales floor when it was offered to him.

During my conversations with him, I quickly realized that he belonged on the sales desk, not as the full-time finance manager. He found himself restructuring the deals that the sales manager had put together. He found that the structuring of the desk manager made no sense to salespeople presenting the numbers and less sense to the customer receiving them. After spending a day with him on the sales desk, watching him structure deals and working with the sales staff, I knew he belonged on the desk.

The next day I had the same conversation with the desk manager who had been on the desk for about eight years. I do what I always do; I position myself at the sales desk and watch the interaction between sales manager, sales staff, and customers. I found that the sales managers would put some figures on a work sheet and send the salespeople off to present the figures to the customer with very little interaction between manager and the salesperson. And when a salesperson could not close his or her own deal, he never offered to step in and assist the salesperson. Not only did he not talk to the customer, but also he didn't even call over the salesperson to see why the customer left in the first place.

As I talked more with him, I realized that his expertise was on the finance side of things. He had a love for finance and had been very good at it. I had to ask him the question, "If you love finance so much, why did you move onto the sales desk?"

"I'm not sure why I did," he said. "The finance department comes easy to me." When I took a finance turn on the finance manager's day off, I made $300–$400 more per deal than he did. I asked a second question: "Would you go back into finance if you had the opportunity?"

He looked at me and said, "Would that even be possible? We already have a finance manager, and I'm not sure two of us can make money with the sales volume here." I said to forget about sales volume for a moment. I repeated the question: "If you had the chance, would you move into the finance office?" He looked at me and said, "Yes, I would!" With a slight pause he then said, "The last few months I have been inquiring about finance jobs at other dealerships."

I asked him if he had ever talked to the owner of the dealership about how unhappy he was at his current role. He said, "Yes, a few times, but the owner told me to stay in my role as a sales manager and that over time I would grow to like it."

Three days later, I gave the sales manager the finance position and moved the finance manager to the sales desk. By the end of that very week, two things happened: My sales volume and front-end gross increased by $600 a unit, and my finance department increased by almost $500 a unit, increasing the total gross over $1,100 per unit. But this was not the best part of switching the managers. The best part was that I now had all the right people doing the right jobs.

The above example illustrates that broken thoughts apply in many ways, and not all of them are obvious. The owner of the dealership made the simple mistake of not being in touch with the employees enough to see that some of them were not satisfied with their roles in the company. Managing personnel to ensure that every employee is working up to full potential is one of the most vital ways to boost productivity, profitability, and customer satisfaction.

As you begin to analyze your dealership, welcome the opportunity to change what isn't working. Change may not be easy, but if change is needed in any or all departments, then action on your part is required. If you give in to inertia, there's no way to grow the business. If you're courageous enough to do what's necessary, then you can goose the throttle and speed to the success you so richly deserve.

CHAPTER 2

THE THREE-CAR SYSTEM

The sales floor is obviously hugely important in any dealership. After all, if you're not moving vehicles, you're losing money. So, it's natural to begin your analysis of the business at the front of the dealership. That's where I always start with the implementation of what I call my three-car system. Usually, sales triple once the system is in place, and everyone is selling the same way with a solid emphasis on maximizing profits in every department. The system is quite simple, but it requires more up-front work from the salesperson and sales management team. It also requires you to think differently about how you run the company.

The genesis of the three-car system goes all the way back to 1984. At the time, I was selling cars on the showroom floor for a dealer in Massachusetts. The dealership's selling process was much the same as the processes I discover in most stores today where dealerships are underperforming and need turning around.

Customers are met on the lot or in the showroom. The salesperson greets the customers with a firm handshake and invites them into the showroom to get a little more information. At this point, hopefully the salesperson gets contact information and determines what the customers really want in a vehicle. Three minutes later, the salesperson is trying to "land them on a car."

The automotive business was changing fast in the 1980s, and yet the same old selling process was not changing much at all. We essentially went into each possible transaction with blinders on. It became quite apparent to me that the sales process needed more than having the salesperson simply select a vehicle and pray that the sales process would work out just fine. It usually didn't. Something always came up to throw a monkey wrench into the workings of the deal. When customers walk away, nobody wins.

It seemed to me that it made no sense to pray that we steered customers to the right car with the hope that they had no negative equity on their trade-in. It struck me as silly to ignore good or bad credit until the question came up toward the end of the deal, only to find out that there was an issue. How could we pick out the right vehicle to maximize the term payment and the cash down payment?

I was sick of spending hours with customers only to find out that I was showing them the wrong vehicle. And the worst part was that the management had no idea about what vehicles we should be showing the customers. How could they know? They knew less about the customers than I did!

The old lot walk and "keep them on one vehicle" was starting to blow up in our faces. I remember the sales manager telling me, "Land them on one car and one car only, and when you get back from the demo ride, start closing them." That was always fun—giving a customer figures with no idea of what reaction I was going to get. I'm not saying we didn't have plenty of questions to ask. I'm just saying there had to be a better way to talk about everything up front with the customer.

I realized that a better sales process was needed, one that clearly cut through all the unnecessary negotiation between the salesperson and the customer. I understood that the sales process shouldn't be totally focused on price alone, but that it should be guided by the customers selecting a vehicle that met their needs and fit their budget. Choosing the finance term versus leasing should have been included in the conversation, but the focus should not have been on price alone.

If there was sincere communication between the salesperson and the customer, then a deal was more likely to happen because stumbling blocks would be identified ahead of time. This would be good for customers, and it would make it possible for the salesperson and management team to maintain full control over the deal.

In addition, I noticed that the sales process differed among the sales staff. Nobody approached the process with a consistent technique. The three-car system is all about consistency in the sales process. It's about having the sales staff approach customers in a uniform manner, all with the idea of maximizing profits for the finance and service departments. Aside from consistency in sales techniques, the three-car system depends on nonconfrontational selling. This system is all about letting the customer compare multiple deals and finance options side by side. In many ways, the three-car system turns the traditional sales process upside down.

On a good day, I'd chat customers up enough to get them on a test drive. If they liked a vehicle enough to want to drive it, I figured I was on my way to making a deal that would go through. At all costs, I'd stay away from talking price, payment, rate, terms, and trade-in value. After the test drive, I'd start asking some closing questions.

- Me: So other than price, is there anything that would stop you from buying this car today?
- Customer: No, price is the biggest concern. I really love the car! I'm just not sure I can afford it.
- Me: I'm sure my manager can work something out. There is usually a certain amount of flexibility. Would you like to know more?
- Customer: Okay, that sounds great. But I'm telling you, I don't think I can afford the car.
- Me: Don't be so sure! There's usually a way to make things happen for you!

At this point, the real work began. Price, the trade-in value, any balance owed on the trade-in, the desired amount of the monthly payment, the cash down payment, and the credit score were now on the table for negotiation. If we got that far, the deal usually went through. With some dealers, the salesperson focuses on price and lets the business manager work out rate, term, and payment in the finance department. Negotiation varies from store to store, but they seem to follow the same path. Some figures go on a work sheet, almost always on just one car with a few terms and payments.

This is where the process falls apart 80 percent of the time. You ask why? I could give you one hundred scenarios, but let's look at three simple ones. Each scenario played out at that dealership in Massachusetts everyday, and as we lost sales, I began to formulate the basis of the three-car system, a sales process that lets the customer drive the deal as much as possible, while the salesperson acts as a sort of guide to subtly steer the customer to the right vehicle and payment structure.

A Dealer Scenario

Say you made the deal and now find out the customer is on the *wrong* car due to his *negative* equity. Do you now try to show that person something different three or four hours into the deal? Do you give up $3,000 of gross in hopes of getting the deal financed through the bank? Now that you showed him or her the *wrong* car, will he or she even stay and listen? Could this have been avoided? Should we have given more choices up front? Was there a way to start the deal from the beginning so that we wouldn't be in this predicament?

The three-car system is based on customer feedback right from the start. It's up to the salesperson to find out what the customer really wants and can afford, thereby decreasing the odds of showing the wrong car.

What if we are on the so-called "right car" and the trade value is somewhat in line with the payoff, but now we run the credit and it's a five hundred credit score? If we quote payments, what was the rate? Is this now a subprime loan; is he or she on the right year and make for term? Do we start the process over again? Did we lose trust at this point? Do we have to bump their payment up $100 or $200 from the initial quote? Could this have been avoided? Is there a process that we missed? This happens a lot more than your staff will let on. In sales, surprises are something you don't want!

What if the customer has a great credit score and no negative equity and loves the car the salesperson showed him or her? Sounds good so far until the customer looks up and says to his or her spouse, "It's about a hundred a month more than we wanted to spend." Do we discount the new or used vehicle to get to the right payment? Do we keep adding money to the trade-in to reach a lower payment? What about asking for more cash down, which they may not be able to come up with for days, weeks, or months? Do we wait for their tax refund?

Now that we know we are on the wrong car, where do we go from here? Do we bring the customer back on the lot and start over? Do we rework the deal on a less expensive car that fits the payment, term, and cash down?

In these cases, customers could always swallow a much larger payment than they had hoped for, but was there still room to sell them products in the finance office? How did we focus them on a vehicle so far away from the monthly payment they were capable of? Was there a better way? Did we lose trust with the customer at this point? Would the vehicle's front end and finance gross profit look a little different if we had the right information from the very beginning? Could this have been avoided with a good process that was done correctly every time?

I saw this sort of thing go on all the time back in 1984, and I still see it happening in stores today. The inefficiency costs dealerships tens of thousands of dollars in lost sales, zero profit for the service and finance departments, and likely no repeat business in the future. And yet, all this could be avoided with an alternative approach like the three-car system that puts the customer in the driver's seat while empowering the sales staff and management.

The alternative approach here is simple. Have a system that gets the sales staff all the information up front. Find out the customer's current monthly payment, balance owned on the trade, how much cash he or she can put down, and his or her credit score, if possible. The most important first step in the three-car system is getting the information we need to allow the salesperson to show vehicles that the customer can actually afford.

A Word on Computers

Computers and software never take the place of a well-executed selling system. In today's automobile dealership environment, we seem to be buying more and more software programs to help us manage our staff. When we purchase the software or new programs, we hope to get state-of-the-art reports and to help guide our staff in the ever-changing buying process. Managers are in some cases very passive and so involved in managing data and statistics that the actual job description gets lost in the shuffle. People, not computers, drive sales.

As a consultant for car and truck dealerships, I've pretty much seen everything. For example, I've seen top management fixate on charts and graphs for every part of the business. Yet, the store was way underperforming and had been for fifteen years! The managers had all the data to show just how badly the company was doing, and they still did nothing to change things for the better even though they had the analytical data to fix the problems. The trouble in this type of dealership began right at the top, and then it trickled down to the staff.

Analyzing Performance

Let's dig a little deeper into the dealer scenario to see how top management dropped the ball. Was it bad staff, wrong location, and poor car line? The staff spent hours looking at this data and analyzing it five ways to Sunday but still had no success. Okay, so it's not the team; they probably have one of the best car lines in the industry, so that can't be it. So I bet you're thinking what I'm thinking: It must be the location of the dealership, poor advertising, or a combination of both.

The town that this "premium car line" was located in had about 9,000 people living in it, but the surrounding town had about 22,000 people. In fact, there were little towns sprinkled all around the dealership from a population of 7,000 to the largest city/town population of over 200,000. So I know what you're thinking now: They're not spending enough money to get the walk-in traffic, or the type of advertising they're doing is not competitive in the marketplace.

So the advertising budget is a great place to start. Most dealers think ad dollars can float or sink a business, and that's true, at least to a certain extent. So, we'll look at the ad budget, and then we can move on to see if the store was aggressive enough in competitive pricing.

Budget: Let's say we moved the numbers from 60 units to 100, and in most months we spent the same or a little less on advertising. In a short amount of time, we moved the store from 100 units to 140 units with about the same budget. Then the dealership sold 160 units, and we spent even less per unit. So it is safe to say it's not the amount of money this store was spending on advertising that drove sales.

Aggressive pricing: I find that it is never aggressive pricing that holds a store back from high volume but a poor understanding of how and why you price. In this case, the store's advertised pricing was competitive in the marketplace from what I could see. The type of advertising could have been improved, and location and layout was not the best, but still it really wasn't all that bad. In fact, it was better than some of the "same like" manufacturers in the market.

So I spent the first day like I always do, counting ups, looking at the inner workings of the deal, and checking if the selling process is done the same way every time. In doing just that, I found out that indeed there was a showroom full of floor traffic to sell lots more new and used vehicles. I also found that the sales process was not only different with every salesperson but with every manager, depending on what the salesperson told the sales desk and who was working the deal.

In a traditional selling dealership, it's all about landing the customer on a vehicle and then discounting till the customer says yes. On paper, the traditional selling process works, but unfortunately, that system falls apart during the introduction when the customer walks up to a vehicle and says, "Let's take this one for a ride." And with no up-front info, the salesperson throws a dealer plate on the vehicle and goes for a test drive.

I compare that to a real estate agent showing million-dollar homes without knowing what the customer's budget is. Think of this, the couple loves the house, the pool, the riding stable, and the game room. The kids pick out their rooms, and the wife has started visualizing where furniture would be placed in each room. The customer says to the realtor, "Let's make an offer for $250,000!" The realtor says,

"That house is listed for $1 million, down from the asking price of $1.1 million."

Tell me this: How is the relationship going now? What house in the $250,000 range will compare to what they looked at? My bet is that they will find a new real estate agent who will work the deal backward. It's just like the three-car system—wants, needs, have-to-haves, and budget. My bet is that the new agent will have three or more homes to compare, all of them financially reachable for the customer.

So, from very early on in my career in automotive sales, I knew that the traditional way of doing things had some serious flaws. I knew when I shopped for things, I liked choice versus limited offers. I liked feeling that I had made the decisions based on comparing all my options and picking the one that worked for me, not one that someone was trying to sell me because it was a deal. In fact, the harder someone tried to sell something, the more pushback he or she got from the customer, even if it was a great deal and the customer wanted to buy.

There's an old saying: If the deal is too good to be true, then something must be wrong. People get suspicious if you try too hard to sell them. In fact, the three-car system is all about making it possible for the customers to sell themselves on the car they want. We're just along for the ride, so to speak.

Did you ever make a ridiculously low offer on a car just to get the sale, and the customer walked away? Was the offer so ridiculous that the customers would have to go home and think about it? The same customer would come back into your dealership a week later and buy something else for more money with fewer options, leaving you scratching your head and asking, *why?* Was the deal too good to be true or was the deal just pushed too hard with no built-in value? People will pay more money for something they think they can't get every time.

Do you remember the Cash for Clunkers program that the government ran a few years ago to get rid of the old gas-guzzling vehicles? It gave customers a big rebate toward a fuel-efficient vehicle. The more mpg the new car got, the more the rebate was. In a short time, we sold out of four-cylinder, fuel-efficient vehicles, and we had people offering over list to get one. The saving really wasn't that much of a deal—there were no programs or discounts, and most of the time, you couldn't even get your color.

The funny part is that months after the program ended, people traded these cars back in for SUVs because they didn't like what they had purchased. People purchased them because the dealer didn't have to sell the deal. It was just the fact that they had one to sell! First come, first served! Sales is a strange game. It's about product, but it's also a lot more about human nature.

CHAPTER 3

INDIFFERENCE

Indifference means you don't care. Intuitively, you'd think indifference doesn't belong in sales, but it actually does. When I go into a dealership to turn it around, I look at every aspect of the company to analyze how each department works in tandem with the others to maximize profitability. One of the first things I do is observe the sales staff, and I'm looking for specific techniques and consistency of approach. Quite often I find that salespeople are anything but indifferent in terms of how they handle customers. They try too hard to sell the deal as opposed to letting the customers sell themselves on the deal.

Let me explain. We all know we should care about customers—we should never be indifferent to them. But we shouldn't come off as pushy either. We're not selling "the deal," but we are selling an understanding of what the customer perceives as value.

Indifference selling is more of a style of selling rather than a process. It's designed to run along the three-car system simultaneously while letting the customer choose his or her path of purchase without being pushed into the deal. The salesperson collects all the right information up front so he or she knows that whatever scenario the customer picks, it will never be price or payment that stops the customer from moving forward.

Some dealers have asked me, "If my salespeople 'sell with indifference,' does that mean they have no option either way?" That's not correct. The indifference style lets them be natural on the deal until they look at all the options. To see all the options before jumping to conclusions is better for the customer and the dealership. Let's take a look at leasing for a moment. It'll help make the point about indifference in sales.

- Salesperson: Have you ever thought of leasing?
- Customer: No, I'd never lease. Leasing is just renting the car.

Now, let's add a dash of indifference to the same conversation.

- Salesperson: I know some people would never consider leasing, and I'm not sure if leasing is going to be the best way to go for you. But with a zero-percent money factor and large rebate, more and more people are looking at it. Let's not rule it out. I'll have my manager run the figures both ways just to make sure you're getting the best deal.
- Customer: Well, I suppose it can't hurt to look at all the options.
- Salesperson: Absolutely! We can run the numbers on buying versus leasing to see what is best for you.

In negotiation, it's dangerous to take sides or pick scenarios up front. It's always better to run them all the way through the bottom line and let the customer pick which one works for him. The question is this: How can we sell from this indifference selling style and do it the same way with each customer? How can we make sure that the sales team is building value and options and giving a clear choice?

Selling the Deal

Let's go into more detail on selling the deal. Picture this. A salesperson walks through the inventory; she is giving the customer information based on incentives and rebates and what she thinks she has the best shot on selling. Nothing is terribly wrong with this style other than that the last three dealerships the customer visited did it the same way, and he still hasn't purchased anything. The salesperson is sharp enough to talk about leasing, cash down, current monthly payment, and trade. And the customer is listening but apparently not ready to buy.

- Salesperson: Would you consider buying a lower cost model? If you did, you could just add leather and it could save you lots of money.
- Customer: No, I only want the model I'm looking at now. If I can't get it, then I'll just keep my present car.
- Salesperson: Well, we have a really nice pre-owned model. It's a one-year certified, and it's at the price you're looking for.

- Customer: No, I only buy new cars. I don't want to buy someone else's problems. Why would anyone trade after a year?
- Salesperson: It's a former rental, and it has a great certified warranty on it—longer than the new one for $5,000 more.
- Customer: I'm not buying a car that had hundreds of drivers. I have seen how people drive rentals, and it's not good.

The salesperson continues to sell the deal! The harder the salesperson pushes the customer on a particular scenario, the more resistance the customer will exert. Some salespeople and managers believe that big discounts and low prices make deals. There are no shortcuts or substitutions for a good process. How many times have you seen a salesperson come to the desk and say, "They already drove the vehicle at the other dealership. They just want to know if we will beat the other dealer's given price"? Why do we have to beat the price? They wanted the local dealer to beat the price because there was no value shown to the customer other than price.

The salesperson had the right idea on talking about moving down a few models and only adding what the customer really wants. An example could be that the customer wanted a limited, but the only options he or she cared about were that it had leather and heated seats. Why pay the $5,000 in limited upgrades if the customer only wanted those two things that cost about $1,500?

- Salesperson: Most of my customers who have been looking at the XYZ Limited have chosen to buy only the XYZ non-Limited and save a ton of money. They figured out they can save thousands and get what they want without paying for things they don't use. My last customers just needed leather and heated seats, so they saved about $3,500, and we did the work right here at the dealership. They even added heated rear seats for the kids and still saved a bunch of money.

- Customer: Maybe we should look at that too.
- Salesperson: I wouldn't rule it out, but I think we should look at both of them to see where the value is.

Let's move on to the indifference selling on the pre-owned rental. The salesperson was trying to give an option by selling on price, not on value. It could have ended up a little different with indifference selling techniques.

The salesperson wanted to offer a certified pre-owned that was a former rental but doesn't want to come off like he's selling the deal. The customer comes in to purchase a new vehicle. He always buys a new vehicle and would never even think of purchasing a used one. So when the salesperson asks the question, the answer is always the same as in the above example. What about asking with indifference?

- Salesperson: You may have seen some of the ads on TV or the paper on our certified program, so I just wanted to go over it so you understand how it works. There are certain vehicles that qualify for a seven-year, 100,000-mile warranty with free roadside assistance and low finance available with great terms. You will find that their prices are between $3,000 and $5,000 cheaper than the new one with a longer warranty.

  There's not a lot of them because they have to pass a crazy factory safety check that can fail most vehicles from becoming certified. In fact, the manufacturer makes us perform a special certified process that even involves a complete history check for past recalls, accidents, and registration data. We purchase a lot of them from XYZ Rental Company. They really take great care of their vehicles, and we handpick only the best part of their fleet. I'm not sure this is for you, but we shouldn't rule it out. I will pull one up just for comparison purposes only; you might as well look at it while you're here.

Indifference selling is how we go about explaining the offers rather than blurting them out. Indifference selling is *staying natural* on selection and keeping the customer open to compare all options. Indifference selling brings the customer down a road of options without giving them a defined opinion. This changes the relationship between the customer and salesperson from someone trying to sell something the customer doesn't want, to someone guiding them through an educational process of choosing the option that fits the customer best. That's the beauty of the three-car system!

Consistency Matters

Consistency in approach is a vital part of the three-car system. When I'm analyzing a dealership's operations, I always look for consistency in sales technique. I always tell the dealer general manager to ask the following questions by dividing the salespeople, desk managers, closers, and finance people into small groups. It's even better if you can interview each person one on one!

Keep the managers apart in order to get a true idea of what each player has to say about the question below. If the responses are all different, then you know you don't have a true system. If you have multiple answers from your manager team, then your manager staff can't be working the deals the same way every time. When I talk about working the deal the same each time, I'm talking about consistency in the sale process. You can't run a sales team with everyone on a different process.

Make sure you have one-on-ones with your salespeople; it may take some time to do this, but it has to be done in order to get a grasp on the sales process. If you find each of them having his or her own sales process that "works for him or her," then that's another disconnect in the sales team. Then pull your finance managers aside one by one to see what they think the process is. If it's different from the sales manager and salespeople, then that's a third disconnect.

Don't get mad at your staff; it's very common that everyone has an individual spin on how it should be done. You will find the process is different depending on the desk manager, the sales manager, and which salesperson gets involved with the customer. Here are some basic questions to ask your staff.

Ask Your Managers

1. When a customer is shopping a like vehicle and has best price and a few lowballs from your competitors, how do you handle it? What system is in place?
2. How do you make your customer feel like he or she got all of his or her shopping done in just one visit?

3. How does your salesperson know what vehicle to show to maximize gross profit?
4. When do you check credit, trade payoff, and negative equity?
5. When should your desk manager first meet the customer?
6. What's the plan from the very beginning?
7. Who's part of the plan? Is it just the salesperson?
8. Did the management team lay it out from start to finish?
9. What is the plan based on, and how did you get the info to put the plan in place?
10. How do you show a lease, used, certified car every time?
11. What do you structure your deal around?

Ask Your Sales Staff

1. What happens when the customer walks in the door?
2. What questions do you ask the customer, and what you do with that information? Do you share it with a manager? If you share it with a manager, at what point do you do that?
3. What determines which vehicles you present to the customer?
4. How do you determine the customer's budget?
5. Is there a process to determine the customer's rate and terms?
6. When do you have the trade appraised?

7. Do you get a payoff on the trade from the bank or do you just use the information the customer gives you? If you get the payoff from the bank, when did you get it? Where were you in the sale process when you got that information?

8. When is the first time that your customer meets a manager?

9. What happens when the customer says no?

10. How many cars do you show?

11. How many test drives do you take?

12. When you give the numbers to the customer, what's on the work sheet? Is it just on one vehicle or is it on multiple vehicles?

13. Do you show lease payments on every work sheet?

Ask Your Finance Manager

1. What do you think the sales process is for the salesperson when he gets a customer?

2. How does the desk determine rate and term when working a deal?

3. When do we check credit?

4. When do we get the payoff on the trade?

5. Who picks out the vehicle for the customer to drive?

6. How does the salesperson know what to show the customer?

7. What's the desk manager's responsibility in the sales process?

8. What are your responsibilities in working the deal?

Now that you have interviewed your staff, it's time to compare notes! With the data you collected, try to map out the sales process from each perspective. For instance, if you make a flowchart on the sales process, does each team follow the process? If you draw a line on a piece of paper following each person's sales process, how many times does it connect?

If your team is like most sales forces, you will see the area of disconnect right away. When talking to your team, be aware that you may get canned responses. What you really want are responses to the above questions that show a deep understanding of why consistency in approach is important, and why the sales process is effective.

As I said, you are looking for the *why* we do it, and *when* we do it rather than labeling the list of steps. Understanding *why* you do a step is the most important part of the selling process; it allows for a plan of attack for your team. When you understand the why, your team can start formulating a plan between the salesperson, desk manager, and closer/floor manager if you have one.

The three-car system is like playing a game of chess. You should know your next move three or four moves ahead of time. An example of this would be your desk manager giving the salesperson a vehicle to show the customer, and the team is looking for a "no" from the customer so they can land the customer on the right car, which is best for both you and them. It's about having a solid plan up front rather than a sales process that few will ever follow every time. Don't get me wrong. All good selling systems have processes that need to be followed, but don't get lost in the process steps. It is not as important as the why and when.

Let's dig a little deeper. First, we'll take a look at a crucial part of the sales process, that time when first impressions are made as a customer walks through the door. We all know the different style salespeople that we employ and all the habits (good and bad) that can get formed over time. Some salespeople like to meet them out in the lot, while others like to wait till they walk into the showroom. Some dealerships have an up system and a greeter, while others just have an open-floor up system.

For the purpose of discussion, let's say it's an open floor. The customer is meeting the salesperson, who has a neat appearance and a big welcoming smile, and who is free of sunglasses, coffee in hand, or any tobacco product.

The plan is not to start walking around aimlessly looking for a vehicle. The plan is that we need to get the right information in order to put a strategy together. The questions below are included on what I call the Quick Sheet, a form sales staff use to get the preliminary information they need before they can properly serve their customers.

The Quick sheet has been designed to start the deal in the right direction by getting some fast facts from the customer. It's all about starting off with a complete understanding of what options we should present to the customer. It's about having a game plan based on facts, not on opinions from our salespeople of what they would do.

Quick Sheet Questions

- What's the current monthly payment, if there is one?
- How much cash was put down last time?
- A trade description, if trading. If not, find out what is happening with it.
- Payoff on the trade, assuming the customer still owes the bank.

- A quick five-liner credit application so we can see what programs we should talk about.
- A customer-need analysis so we can separate the "have to have" from the "would love to have but don't need it."

These are the only things we really need from the customer, and we need them all upfront before we start showing the wrong vehicles. Most customers come in thinking they know exactly what they want—color, options, and price. And we give them everything they want, including the deal they asked for!

But why is it when it's time for them to take out the checkbook, they say to the salesperson or manager, "We still have to shop around, but if we buy something, it will be from you"? That's because, in reality, the customer only has a *perception* of what he or she wants.

That's why the Quick sheet is so important. The first thing the salesperson does is sit down with the customer with the Quick sheet. The objective is to get answers to all six questions—and, yes, we get this info almost 100 percent of the time. You may be thinking that your customer would never sit down and give this info to your salespeople. Rest assured, they will! With the right training, they all give us the info upfront. Worst case possible, you may have to answer a few questions first, then sit them down and get the Quick sheet.

So how long do you think it takes for a salesperson who is comfortable with the Quick sheet to get the information from the customer and up to the sales desk? Let me start by saying this: If the salesperson is not up at the desk looking to create a plan with the desk manager in about ten to fifteen minutes, then there is a problem. This is not something that takes twenty or thirty minutes. All this is a fact-finding mission for us so we can start the right plan from the very beginning.

When I'm training a new salesperson to use this, I actually jot down the time on a customer log sheet when the salesperson starts the Quick sheet with the customer. That gives my desk and closing manager a time guide to see if the salesperson is spending too much time or not enough time on the fact-finding mission. Either way, it's all about managing the deal from start to the finish. Think about this: For the first time, your salesperson is showing vehicles that are in the price range of what the customer wants. Your team is in control and putting their plan in place from the very start of the process.

This process takes 100 percent focus from your sales staff; it's a full commitment from start to finish on every deal. Remember that the focus doesn't mean selling the deal itself. Instead, it's important to apply the technique of indifferent selling as the sales staff guides the customer to closing by presenting options that present a value proposition that fits the customer's needs and budget.

CHAPTER 4

OVERCOMING OBJECTIONS

The most successful sales teams require active managers. Managers must be willing to interact with customers during the sales process. I find if a manager comes over and chats with the customer, he or she can get a second opinion on what the plan is going to be on the sales desk.

Let's face it; in most dealerships, they don't meet any member of the management team until there is a problem with the offer or lack of one. If the salesperson needs help or direction, he doesn't have to leave his customer and go back to the sales desk. The manager can help put him or her back on track if needed.

So now we get the Quick sheet info: current payment, cash down, trade, VIP sheet (credit), payoff, and need analysis. Now it's time to bring the information to the desk manager so that person can start a plan on the best possible vehicle to show the customer. Most customers want to be around the same payment as they're paying now, and with the same cash down or less. That's why it's important for the selection process to have this info.

From this point forward, your team will be working all your deals backwards. That's right, within five minutes, you will put a quick figure on the trade and take a snapshot of the credit with a VIP sheet. Having all of this info upfront makes it simple to back into a payment that's comfortable for the customer.

Even if we need more cash down or longer terms, it's better to start having that dialogue with customers up front. I'm not saying we tell them no, this can't give you what you want. We just give options and let them pick which one fits them best.

What if a customer is totally unrealistic on what he or she perceives on price and payment due to his or her situation? Let's take a look at two examples of an unrealistic demand from a customer due to the two big elephants in the room: credit and negative equity. Both of these conditions could affect the new monthly payment or terms of the deal. Both can kill a deal, if you let it happen.

The three-car system is multi-layers of small processes that help the deal continue to move forward, despite any obstacles that may arise. Your sales team is getting all the information needed to start off the sales process on the right foot. Within the first ten minutes, the customer is going to meet a manager with a warm greeting.

The purpose of the manager coming over so early in the deal is to make sure the salesperson is heading in the right direction. Using this approach up front, you will have the customer's current monthly payment, cash down, payoff on trade, and trade description in the first ten minutes of meeting your customer. Your manager will also have a good idea of trade value and the wants and needs of the customer. Information is the key to offering the customer the right options that can lead to closing a deal.

Unrealistic Demands

The customer tells the salesperson that he or she wants the same $300 payment that he or she is paying now, and he or she only has $1,000 to put down. When the salesperson asks the customer if money is owed on the trade, the customer says yes and gives the salesperson a roundabout figure.

Of course, it's vital to confirm the payoff amount before moving on. If the payoff is more than we thought, who eats it? The customer? My bet is if it means the payment is going up or we need more cash down, nine times out of ten, it comes out of the deal's gross profit and not the customer's pocket. That's why getting information up front with the Quick sheet is so important.

Then the customer gives us the list of options and features and demands in order for it to be worth it to trade up into something new. Salespeople with great experience can sometimes see that they're heading in the wrong direction from the very beginning with what the customer wants versus what the customer is willing to pay and can afford.

With no system in place, the salesperson comes to a fork in the road. Do I (a) explain to the customer who insists on keeping his current monthly payment with only $1,000 down with all that negative equity that this is impossible to do? This means that in the first five minutes after I meet this person, I'm telling him it can't be done. Or (b) do I show him what he wants and hope that he is willing to pay a lot more? The salesperson then takes that customer out in the lot test-driving vehicles that are not even close to his budget.

While all of this is going on, the customer forgot to mention that his credit score this time around has dropped two hundred basis points from the last time he applied for an auto loan. Even worse, the customer had no idea that the credit had dropped two hundred basis points, and it wasn't from a lack of making payments on time, it was from the amount of revolving credit that was available to him.

So the deal goes on. The new salesperson or the one who hates dealing with confrontation tends to take road (b) and waits until the end of the deal to spring all of this on a manager after two hours have gone by between service walks and demo rides. Do you think the manager wants to go out to this mess and try to piece a deal back together? If your desk manager has three other deals working, do you think he's going to give this one his all? Do you think we could have done something different here? The short answer is yes.

Working Deals the Smart Way

Traditionally in most dealerships, we show the customer what he or she wants up front after getting very limited information. Trust me on this one, more times than not, the manager has to get involved because the deal is not moving forward. The manager starts off with an apology on why we can't be at their numbers and terms. At that point in the deal—which is way too late in the process—the manager is trying to figure out what the right vehicle is to show the customer to get the best terms.

With the right information, you can identify objections and overcome them before things fall apart. It really is common sense, but a surprising number of dealerships drop the ball before the process even gets started! It's all about moving forward to the next step with the customer in the process. Think about it. How many times have you seen a salesperson come to the desk and say, "I have nothing here. They're out of time and have to go to an appointment!"

So you send a manager into the deal to talk to the customer, and wow, ten minutes later they're still talking. Fifteen minutes later, the manager has the salesperson pull up an altogether different vehicle from what the salesperson was showing in the beginning. Forty-five minutes later, they're signing contracts in the business office and taking delivery of the customer's new vehicle.

So, what happened here? How did the manager get the customer to stay and continue to move forward in the deal-making process? What made the manager change vehicles and offer something different? Why did the customer tell the salesperson they had to leave and would come back?

Let's start with the first question: *How* did this happen? And then let's see if we can start connecting some crucial missteps of a traditional process versus the three-car system. The first question is easy for me to answer. The customer wasn't hearing what he needed to hear in order to move to the next step. In fact, the salesperson didn't have a true understanding of what the customer wanted so they were stuck in the process and couldn't move forward. The salesperson was selling the deal, not presenting the customer with a value proposition.

After some uncomfortable conversation between the customer and salesperson, guess what? Surprise, the customer was out of time and had to go. The customer was never out of time, just out of patience with the whole process and misdirection from the salesperson.

The manager who took over the deal for the salesperson took the time to find out the right information to see if they were even on the right vehicle. The second thing was to outline a plan for the customer on how to get what he wanted. The third thing the manager did was offer multiple ways for the customer to achieve goals in these categories: price, payment, trade value, and options.

By doing this, the manager started winning over the customer in small segments of the selling process. The three-car system is multi-layers of small processes that help the deal continue to move forward. The multi-layer part of the process has to do with winning the customer over with small victories, one small part at a time.

By doing this, we are in constant forward motion in the selling process rather than fighting our way point to point on the sale process. This all ties in with indifference selling and empowering your salespeople with a tool to guide them through this nonconfrontational selling system.

When salespeople meet the customer on the three-car system, they're not thinking about selling a vehicle; they're thinking about selling the next step of the sales process. With traditional selling systems, it's easy for salespeople to make a quick assumption on whether they have a deal or not. If you have a salesperson who cannot get anyone in the showroom, my bet is that this is what's going on.

Between poor body language and lack of a real process, I have seen sales staff meet-and-greet five to six customers out in the lots and never even come close to coming inside. Of course if you ask them, customers didn't have any time to look around right then, but they would be coming back next week when they had the time.

Isn't it funny that customers drive all the way to dealerships just to spend ten minutes with a salesperson so they can get back into their cars and leave? This ties in with the example we just talked about. The uncomfortable conversation between the customer and salespeople, and surprise! The customer was out of time and had to go.

Every person in the lot has to get logged. There are lots of ways of doing this. I find keeping all the deal folders behind the sales desk works best. Every time your salesperson gets a customer, he or she needs to go to the sales desk first to get the folder. Two things happen here: First, the manager now can log the customer, and second, he can make sure the salesperson enters the customer in whatever front-end tool your dealership has for follow-up.

Every Quick sheet needs to be numbered at the top so they can get an accurate idea of how many customers make it to this point. At the start of each month, you need to number the Quick sheets. These will be kept at the sales desk so the salesperson has to go to the desk to get one. This lets the managers know that there is a deal working, and the floor manager should be getting ready for the first flyby T.O. with the customer.

It is important to do this as often as possible because it keeps the salesperson in check and lets the customers know we are there to help guide them along the process. In most stores, they only meet a manager when they say no or make an offer that's too low. When the customer sees the salesperson come back with a manager at his or her side during the negotiation process, he or she always has that same look—the "here we go" look.

That is why the flyby T.O. is so important to build the trust and say hi to the customer before the selling process starts. And it's always better going into a deal that you already established some common ground with the customer. Doing so will help you overcome any objections that come up as the sales process continues.

The following steps will help sales staff avoid mistakes that lead to objections that can kill a deal. As you can see, there's a bit of paperwork involved, but it won't take long.

In fact, it shouldn't take your salespeople more than ten minutes to get the vital information they need to effectively sell in a nonconfrontational way with the three-car system.

1. Need analysis sheet (half sheet)
2. VIP sheet (five-line credit application)
3. Trade appraisal sheet
4. Quick trade payoff sheet
5. Copy of the driver's license
6. Bring all the above paperwork to the sales manager for selection of vehicles.

We get current monthly payment and cash down, so we still need the trade appraisal, the trade payoff, and a quick look at the credit to see what programs we can offer. When the salesperson sits down with the customer, he asks the customer if it's okay to work the deal backwards.

- Salesperson: We do things differently at this dealership. We want to make sure you have all of your options up front so when you leave here you will have everything you need to make an educated decision about which vehicle to buy. So I'm going to get a little info to help speed up the process. Is that okay?
- Customer: What kind of information?
- Salesperson: Just some basic data we can use to help serve you best. For example, we'd like to run a quick credit check to see what kind of financing we could do for you.
- Customer: I'm not sure I even want to buy a car yet, so why do you need my credit score?

- Salesperson: We find it's best to get the basic information up front. That way we can better serve you. It's important to us that we present you with all the options. Your credit score will help us do that. We have a VIP sheet for you to fill out.
- Customer: Okay, I guess that makes sense.
- Salesperson: Great, then let's begin!

The salesperson is going to get a quick payoff on the trade, which is easily done if you have all the local banks and credit union phone numbers on one sheet of paper. Now the appraisal sheet gets done, and the only other important part left to do is the quick credit sheet. One out of twenty customers will say, "No thanks, my credit is perfect." In those cases, it usually is. So we just keep moving forward and assume they have great credit. If customers object to a quick credit check, don't push them. Just move on.

So, to recap, we have current monthly payment, we have all the trade info, and we have the bank they financed with and the payoff. When we pencil the deal, we will use the same cash down as they put down last time. If the customer's wants and demands are not realistic at this point, you can start shaping the deal with indifference selling up front.

Say the customers want to be at the magic monthly payment of $250 with little to no cash down. They are also $2,000 upside down in their current trade, and they want that paid off. Sounding a little familiar at this point? Hold on, it's going to get worse. They want a $23,000 SUV with a third seat if possible.

On a traditional selling system, we would do two things: (a) start explaining to the customers that it's impossible to get what they want for what they've budgeted for a vehicle, or (b) take them in the vehicle they wanted and start hoping that they're willing to pay a lot more if they fall in love with it.

The Three-Car System in Action

- Salesperson: With $250 a month budget and a little cash down and us paying off your existing loan, we have a lot of options to show you.
- Customer: Terrific!
- Salesperson: On the SUV that you're thinking about, I have seen payments as high as $400 a month depending on the terms of the loan. For some reason over the past year or so, my customers have been taking advantage of a better way to finance the vehicle. Even with super-low rates from the bank and cash down, my customers tell me it is just a much better option than a long-term loan. We call it a smart lease, and the money factor on the one you're looking at is almost zero percent. The finance terms are cut in half versus traditional long-term loans. This may not be for you, but we shouldn't rule it out. We'll look at it later.
- Customer: I'm not interested in leasing.

If the customer objects, take an indifferent stance. Don't push the deal.

- Salesperson: I understand. Lots of people tell me that. Smart leases aren't for everyone. In your case, though, it could be a good option. We'll draw up a couple of plans to show you how you can get the SUV you want.

With the strong lease programs we have today, filling the customer's demands on payment and cash down can be done without giving up front-end gross profit. Overcome the objections and resistance a little at a time with indifference selling techniques. Draw comparisons. Give options. Tell stories to build rapport with customers. As Henry Ford famously said, "People don't sell cars. Stories do!"

CHAPTER 5

ON-THE-JOB TRAINING

The importance of training sales staff cannot be understated. If the staff doesn't know the sales process, they can't sell vehicles, maximize profits in the finance department, or drive business to the service department. The most important skill the salespeople have is the ability to think on their feet. They can't sell the deal. They can't push too hard. They can't approach the process with blinders on.

So, how do you incorporate this innovative kind of selling into your dealership? Do you sit people down in a classroom? Or do you go with a more intuitive hands-on approach? I bet your top sales and service people are thinking on their feet right now without even knowing they're doing it.

A customer asks them a question about a certain situation or problem, and they answer it with a comparison of what the last customer did in the same situation. Because they got great results with the customer situation, they continue to use customer comparisons.

Think about how you like to learn something new. Do you like someone to stand there and tell you what and how to do something? Or would you learn differently if someone had shown you how to do it? Today, the employees learn more in real-life onsite training than in any all-day lecture. It comes down to this: Don't tell me how it's supposed to be done; show me how it's supposed to be done. Don't take my word for it; go to the YouTube search bar and type in "How do I fix a leaky faucet?" Yes, you will have about fifty videos detailing step by step how to fix your faucet.

I find in many dealer groups, both large and small, that we tend to hire a sales trainer to do our training. Usually our sales trainers work directly with our new hires, teaching them our in-house selling process. So let me ask you this question: Why is it that we don't let our sales managers train new people in the process?

Most of you are going to say your management team just does not have the time. Some of you are going to say you want to make sure your new people get the right training so you can retain them long-term. Some of you are going to say, you want the same selling process taught to the new sales staff every time. These are all valid answers, but let's dig a little more with this question.

Have you ever heard from your new hires that training was great and that they learned a lot, and yes they're 100-percent ready to start on the floor? Two days into handling showroom customers, and your new salesperson can't even follow the simplest part of the sales process?

Okay, so what happened to "everyone needs to get the same training program"? Do you think your management staff is spending more or less time with this salesperson who can't follow a process? How's the confidence level of your new salesperson? Do you think you will retain him or her?

Do we really think that we saved any of our management time training new staff in front of the chalkboard for two weeks? If training in a classroom works so well, why is it we only retain about 25 percent of the people even after their training?

Put your thinking cap on for a moment. Do you remember when you first started to sell cars? Did you learn more from someone telling you how it's done or did you learn more when someone actually showed you how to do it? When you have only classroom-trained sales staff, the first time they get in front of a customer and the customer is not willing to play along with the new salesperson's line of questioning, the entire process gets thrown right out the window.

All the role-playing in the world can't prepare a new salesperson for real-life selling situations. Our salespeople who are trained only in the classroom have a hard time starting from a different point in the process due to customers' individual situations. Let me give you a simple example why a classroom salesperson with no actual real-life floor experience is bound to fail.

A customer comes in and says, "Before I do anything or give you any of my information, I want to know what my trade value is." The classroom new hire is at the sales desk in about three minutes and repeats what the customer said.

- New salesperson: The customer will not give me any of his personal information and wants to know what his trade is worth before he looks at anything. He won't even tell me what he's looking at!

What would you have your desk manager do in this situation? The answer is simple. The newly hired salesperson would be told to go with the flow. Skipping a step you can come back to is a better way of overcoming objections than sticking to a script no matter what. With indifference selling, the salesperson lets the customer lead the way. The newly hired salesperson returns to the customer on the sales floor.

- Customer: So, can I get my trade-in value now?
- Salesperson: I checked with my manager, and he says it's fine to start off with finding out what your trade value is. This sounds like it's really important to you.
- Customer: It really is. The money I get back on the car will go right into the new SUV I have my eyes on.
- Salesperson: At this dealership we look at the trade like a separate part of the deal. Is that okay?
- Customer: Yes. So where do we go from here?

Notice that the salesperson didn't pounce on the fact that the customer mentioned wanting a new SUV. Instead, he remained focused on what the customer wants to find out, namely the trade-in value. In this case, the newly hired salesperson hit a home run. If he or she had shifted gears to start selling the SUV, the customer would have become annoyed. It would seem like the salesperson wasn't listening.

- Salesperson: Great! Then let's start. Did you buy your car from a new or used car dealer? What made you pick this one? Was the warranty important when you purchased it? I'm asking because we have used, new, and certified in stock. Do you know what some of the differences between them are?

The difference between the classroom-trained salesperson and the indifference in-house trained salesperson is the ability to start with step 4 in the selling process and still have the ability to finish all the steps.

Indifference selling lets you integrate the selling steps without having to start at step 1 and then go to step 3 and then to step 4. You can start at step 5 and then go to step 2. It's all about having a process that is conducive to always moving forward to the next step. A selling process should never be more important than helping the customer. The process is only part of guiding the customer toward the sale.

In some dealerships, I have seen the sales process become more important than actually helping a customer. A good litmus test to see what kind of selling system you have is to ask your sales staff a few questions. Here are a few that should test your system.

1. If your customer just wants a price, what happens?
2. What if the customer just wants to know what their vehicle is worth?
3. What if the customer just wants to go for a drive?
4. What if the customer wants to know what the best interest rate is before even looking at anything or giving us his or her name?

If the answers to any of these questions finds the salesperson having to come to the desk without the freedom of moving between the steps, then you're selling system is broken. Or should I say, the system has a greater value than the customer!

When in the classroom, the new salesperson is taught a different part of the process each day. Every day the salesperson learns what the next step is, and in most cases role-plays it with fellow classmates. This goes on and on for weeks until the entire sales process is completed. The problem with this kind of training process is that the new salesperson has a hard time following the process if the customer is not willing to play along.

Sales is fluid. The best sales staff can read the customer and respond accordingly, but the salesperson never forgets the process, nor does he or she leave out a step even if the order of those steps shifts around based on the unique nature of each sales scenario.

If your team can't give you the selling process and all be on the same page, then what do you think your new salesperson thinks when he goes to different managers and gets asked to work a deal totally differently every time? Imagine how confused you'd be.

Think about this for a moment. Your new sales candidate comes to the desk, his first time working a car deal, and hears this: "I know that's how 'they' trained you, but we don't work deals that way here." Then the desk manager gives the salesperson his own take on the next step that salesperson should be doing.

The next day, the salesperson works a deal with a different manager on the desk, and the new candidate gets a different selling version than he got from the last manager he worked a deal from. And by the way, each desk manager's version was different from the initial training that the salesperson got just days ago. I see this sort of thing all the time. Lack of consistency in the sales process is a major reason why some dealerships don't reach peak performance.

So, how do you train your complete sales staff, including finance managers and closers, on the same selling system? And better yet, how can you train them to sell with indifference? Consistency in the sales process is the key.

Get the information up front that you need. Skip steps if you have to but make sure to complete every step in the sales process. Don't push the deal. Sell with indifference.

If you're selling cars in the traditional way, it's time to change the way you think when it comes to training your entire sales staff! Think of it as a self-cleaning oven. Every time the process is done, it self-trains the sales staff a little bit at a time. Just by the sales manager using the selling system in a real-life situation, he self-trains his sales staff without spending useless hours in a training room.

Don't get me wrong. The three-car selling system and selling from indifference take some classroom training. But unlike traditional selling systems that have complicated, unrealistic steps that don't work in real-world showrooms, it trains the individual salesperson as he or she is actually selling a vehicle.

You may be wondering why you would waste a good walk-in customer on some new salesperson who going to be training. I will answer that question with another. When your salespeople leave the training class after ten days and start taking walk-in customers, how many walk-ins do you think they go through before they have a true understanding of the process?

If you have a good customer retention management program (CRM) process in place (which most stores do), when you get back to your store, have your manager run a log on each salesperson and how many customers that each is taking. You will find that your new salespeople are taking the lion's share of the walk-in floor traffic. Don't get too worked up on those numbers; it's like that in the majority of dealerships today, big and small.

Becoming Part of the Process

The first step in shifting your dealership from a traditional sales mode to the three-car system is getting your management team on the same page. I find you can't train your salespeople on a selling process unless your management team is fully engaged in it. If your dealership is underperforming, your management team is likely at the root of the problem. Each department should be managed to maximize profits, but that is often easier said than done.

It's very common to see a parts and service portion of the operation prosper, even though the sales department, new and used, have been declining every year. There could be twenty different scenarios on how and why this could happen, but let's talk about what I have seen that is most common in dealer groups that are family-owned.

I'm picking family-owned dealerships because this is where I get my highest volume of calls from dealers looking for help. This call is almost always the same. It's a dealer calling me looking for the understanding to see why the market is doing well in his region, but his ranking has fallen every year, while dealerships in that district seem to be taking the market share away from his dealership.

One of the first things he says to me is that the general manager or sales management has been there for years, and that he has been able to keep the same players on the management team year after year with little-to-no turnover of the management staff. For that, I take my hat off and congratulate the ownership for keeping a stable crew! If the owner of the dealership had promoted its management team over the years, then they must have been successful at one time.

So keeping with the same train of thought, what has happened over time that has made that same team less and less effective over the years? If you're from a big box motor group, I have an idea of what you're thinking. Why would a dealer make no money just to keep the staff? Let me say this: Most family-owned dealers who call me are making money; some of them have millions of dollars fall to the net bottom line every year. So why would they call me if they have a staff that's been in the store for years, and the dealership is making money?

It's common that the service, parts, and body shop in a long-term family owned dealership can be over 100 percent absorption. I had one owner from a Boston dealership tell me this: "If I'm able to pay myself rent and salary, and meet my payroll every week, then my dealerships are successful." I would call that a broken thought, but let's move on.

The dealer ripped open his franchise dealer statement to show me that after he collected his rent, made payroll, took out some a small end-of-year bonus for him and his son, he still had a net profit of $359,000. One of the first things I looked at was the dealer salary; it was on the low side. In fact, most of my top managers made more than the dealer paid himself.

The next thing I looked at was what the dealership was paying in rent. And again, it was less than half the rent that I had seen in that market and location. The dealer's argument was that the land and building had no mortgage; he had paid it off over the past thirty years of ownership.

Then the dealer and I looked at the gross and nets of each department of the dealership. I highlighted each department's gross profit on the top of the statement. Then I circled the nets of each department. We quickly discovered that only two departments carried all the rest of them. I looked at the dealer and told him he had five departments: new cars, used cars, service, parts, and body shop. The dealer nodded his head in agreement. So why did only two out of the five actually make a net profit?

For the next twenty minutes, the dealer explained to me why this had happened. He pointed out that the manufacturer had some product problems over the years. The Internet had crushed his front-end gross profit. He said that it's hard to find the right used cars unless you trade them. When the dealer finally took a breath, I asked him to describe each of the department heads.

The funny thing was when he was talking about the department managers with strong gross and net, he described them the same way: hardworking, lots of hours, and a great attention to detail. When he was describing his department managers that had minimal gross or net profit, out came the broken thoughts. I could see the pain in the dealer's face while trying to justify why his low-gross managers weren't getting the job done. Instead of talking about these managers' skills and attention to detail, he talked about their long-term relationships and his struggle to get them to move forward.

The second thing to do is to get up on the sales desk and become part of every deal that is being worked. You're not going to work the deals; you're there to see how the desk managers and salespeople work them. This is where you get a measurement of how each manager approaches each deal. Let me give you a simple example of what to look for when measuring a manager's understanding of a deal.

When your manager is communicating to the salesperson, what kind of information is he looking for? How did your sales manager approach the deal? What kind of feedback was your sales manager looking for from the salesperson? Did your sales manager give guidance to the salesperson before he or she started showing vehicles? And if they did, what was it, and what was it based on? What was the vehicle selection process, and what determined that? All these questions are very important in analyzing the sales process. If you identify gaps, you can work to fill them.

Okay, let's move on to the sales manager penciling in the deal, to see what his line of thinking is. Does he preload the lips of the salesperson? How does he pencil the deal? Does he offer a lease up front on every deal? Is every deal getting a payment with cash down? Does he hold back on the trade? Does the manager who is penciling the deal have a well-thought-out plan of action? And if he has a plan, does the manager clue in the salesperson as to what's going on, or is he just serving numbers and getting offers with no true understanding of what the plan is?

A well-executed plan by the desk manager and sales staff encourages good gross profits, good customer satisfaction, and same-day delivery. This is where you really get to measure your managers' needs so you can get an understanding if they're a good fit for the new system. Unfortunately, not every manager can adapt to this system. There is a certain type of manager who works well for this program. This is where staff development is so important in picking out the right employees to build your team.

Staff Development

In some cases, when I take over a store that's underperforming, I find that the dealership has great employees who are informative and customer friendly. I also find that they truly want to do the best for the customers and the dealership they work for. So the million-dollar question that I'm asked by almost every dealer principal seems to be about the same every time. They ask, "If I have such great employees working for me, why am I underperforming compared to the other dealers in my market? Why can't they get the job done?"

The dealer, without letting me answer the question, continues on and on with how these employees have been with him for years and are very loyal to him. Then the dealer goes on about how they were sent to training. He has given them all the tools and still they always come up short of their goals.

Unfortunately, the dealer was asking the wrong questions about the dealership staff. There are three stages of questions that need to be asked. The first question is, Why did you promote them? The second question the dealer will have to ask himself is, Do they have the skill set to move their departments forward and hit their team goals? And the third is, If they are in the wrong management role, is there a better place in the dealership for them to excel in?

Question 1: Why was the person promoted?

I was asked to look at an underperforming dealership in a small town in New England. The first day is always the same for me. I watch the interactions between management and staff, and all employees' interactions with customers. Another key component is watching how the staff deals with the customers through other employees.

For instance, when a lower-level employee has a problem with a customer, and you can see that the problem is not getting solved and the customer is getting irritated at this point, what happens here tells an important story. The first hour that I was at a new dealership, I saw this exact situation go down.

It was between a salesperson and a general sales manager who had been there for years. The salesperson was on his third attempt in trying to explain a problem to the manager. You could see the customer twelve feet away from the sales desk with his family, all getting more and more frustrated at every attempt of the salesperson to solve his problem.

The general sales manager was now going to send in another employee to see if he could help smooth out the bad situation that had now been going on for over forty-five minutes. The new problem here was that now a different salesperson, who had nothing to do with the deal other than he was told to "figure it out," was now sent in to solve the problem.

Then voices started to rise and the customer said, "Who are you? I have to start from scratch with you? Do you have to go back to that guy behind the desk or can you make a decision on your own?"

The newly involved salesperson looked back at the manager behind the desk for some kind of direction or help, but all he got back was a blank stare from the manager. Then the general sales manager got up from his desk with his phone in his hand and walked out of the showroom.

When I asked the general sales manager why he didn't just go over and solve the customer's problem himself, he looked at me and said, "I don't like talking to customers. My T.O. manager is off today, or I would have sent him."

What does this tell us? Why did the owner, who was the acting general manager, put this person in a general sales manager position? I watched these kinds of interactions between employees and management go on all day. If this story sounds a little outlandish, think again! There are reasons why dealerships underperform, and this sort of bad communication is one of the most common ones.

So when I drafted my report and reviewed it with the owner, he smiled and said that was why he let him promote a salesperson to be a closer—he hates talking to customers.

So here's the million-dollar question I had to ask the owner: "Then why did you promote him to this level if he doesn't like talking to customers?"

Then the backpedaling started from the dealer. He said it was not that he didn't like to talk to customers; it was that he was never properly trained. The owner went on for a while that this guy was a great employee—never called in sick and was great with handling paperwork with the office if they needed something.

Do you think this was the wrong person to promote to increase sales volume, and train the sales staff on good customer service? Do you think the owner promoted someone who could move the needle? Do you think any level of training was going to make this manager feel comfortable talking with customers? Was a great employee with lots of skills just put in the wrong job? How could we be so disappointed with the manager when the job didn't get done?

Question 2: How do I know that my manager has the skill set to move my team forward?

You can't make people into something they're not. It's safe to say that with the proper training and correct motivation, you can really grow the correct individual into something very special. These are the qualities that I look for in an individual before I consider him or her a team manager.

a. The ability to motivate people in a positive way.
b. The ability to look in the mirror and take full responsibility if something didn't go as planned.
c. Strong work ethic, no such thing as a day off, and no vacation until the job gets done. First one in and last one to leave until the job gets done.

d. A strong passion for what he does and how he does it.

e. The ability to look into an employee's eyes and know that something's wrong.

f. The ability to see when an employee is doing the wrong job or is in the wrong position.

g. Even if an employee is a very good friend, he has the ability to make a change regardless of the end result.

h. Last but not least, the ability to laugh at himself and his mistakes.

The above is a baseline of where to start. Once you establish that you have a manager with these qualities, you can start moving forward with training.

Question 3: If the manager is in the wrong job, is there another role or department that would better suit the person's skill set?

That's not always an easy judgment to make, but I always encourage the owners of a dealership to try to keep good employees. In fact, you can build even better employee loyalty and retention if you work hard to put people in jobs that suit them best. Recall the general sales manager who didn't like talking to people? The owner knew he was happiest doing paperwork and carrying out administrative duties that were necessary to the company. Recall also that a closer was hired to assist sales staff in cementing deals.

The prudent thing to do would be to promote the closer to general sales manager and move the present general sales manager to office manager with no loss of pay. If you spun it the right way, the present general sales manager wouldn't see the move as a demotion.

CHAPTER 6

THE WHOLE DEAL

When I come into a new store, I always have the same approach when it comes to training the sales management team. Once I know I have the right managers in the right place, I start moving forward with training them how to understand the deal. As funny as that may seem, sales managers and general sales managers seem to have a different understanding of what a deal is. Let me give you an example.

I had a sales manager pass on a negative front-end gross deal of $750 on a high-volume model in a particular car line. When I asked the manager why he passed on that deal, he said the owner didn't want them blowing money on new car deals. The customers were taking zero-percent financing and that only paid them a $100 flat fee. What are some of the things that the sales manager should have been looking at?

Let's look at the facts. The customer had a trade and the actual cash value was in line with the market value. The customer was indeed only financing because of the zero-percent interest rate, and his or her credit was excellent. The customer also lived less than five miles from the dealership, and he was on his third "same" make and model vehicle. He had purchased all the others from our competitor twenty miles away.

When we interviewed the customer, he in fact always serviced at the other dealership because he purchased their maintenance plans, and they always give the customer a free loaner car. So back to the questions the sales manager should have been asking himself before he dismissed the deal. With zero-percent financing, how easy would it have been to sell other products?

If the customer was driving twenty-plus miles because of a maintenance plan, could we have sold him one? How easy was it to sell a customer's trade that was three to four years old that had all of its maintenance done versus a vehicle that was a former rental? What would have been the profit of us selling the customer's trade? What would have been the internal shop bills profit on the customer's trade to the dealership? Would the trade have brought us a new sales and service customer and maybe an additional trade?

Understanding a whole deal can make your manager have the ability to make better deal-making decisions. Fortunately, that manager was in training that day and we stopped the customer from leaving the showroom and took that deal. The finance department produced a profit of $1,330, while the customer's trade sold in six days for a front-end and finance department gross profit of $2,644. The repair order on that trade was around $900. The deal actually got better for the dealership, because the second trade sold for a profit of $3,233—and before it hit day three in the lot.

While getting your management team on the same line of thinking is important, when it comes to making a deal, it's as important that they line up in how to price your inventory. When your management team starts getting the whole picture on what makes a deal profitable for the dealership, then they can make a clear decision based on all the facts.

Just to give you an example of how a manager can have the same problem with understanding "the deal" on the retail-selling side, let me give you this scenario: One of my dealerships in which we were installing the three-car system didn't have a sufficient amount of pre-owned inventory. So the pre-owned manager purchased some domestic current-year make and model rentals so we would have something to sell.

This was an import store that sold mostly imports when it came to pre-owned cars. The domestic vehicles were perfect for a customer who was looking for low monthly payments on a vehicle that still was under factory warranty compared to the imports we sold. Besides, the used car manager could buy five or fifty whenever he wanted.

The sales manager and used car manager were working a deal side by side on one of the retails that he just purchased. The salesperson brought up an offer with the credit card on one of the newly purchased rentals. The offer was low so the used car manager went to the customer to try to cultivate a better offer. The used car manager was unable to move the customer in price, so he came back to the desk and said, "I just purchased this car. I don't want to take a $900 deal after shop on this one."

So I asked both managers for their line of thinking on this deal. They both said the same thing: Our average gross profit on a pre-owned is $1,800; why should I take a $900 deal? So I asked them if the customer was financing with us. They both said yes. So I asked the team another question.

What's your average finance profit on a pre-owned vehicle here? They both looked at the daily doc that was printed out each morning and said it's about $1,000 on used vehicles.

So I asked another question. If you sold this rental to this customer, do we have the potential to make $1,900 and deliver a car today? They both shrugged their shoulders and said yes. So here comes the last question: If we sold this rental today, how fast could we get another one just like it here? Without blinking an eye, the used car manager said, "I could have twenty here tomorrow, why do you ask?"

Before I answer that question, I asked how many of these vehicles were in our market in a fifty-mile radius and that were for sale at other dealerships? So both managers looked at the appraisal tool on their desktop computer and clicked the same model type for sale in a fifty-mile radius. They both looked up and told me there were about thirty or so.

As a dealer principal, I can only guess what you're thinking at this moment and the questions you're probably asking yourself. Here are some of my thoughts, and I would like to start at the beginning to give us some clarity of why it's important to understand the whole deal. Understanding the whole deal has nothing to do with holding or giving away gross; it's having the ability to look at a deal from all aspects. For instance, the used car manager would have taken a $1,900 cash deal if someone walked in off the street and wrote out a check. So what was wrong with a $900 gross in the front, and letting the business manager finance and sell service maintenance and extended warranty products?

Passing on the deal would have kept the shop bill of $800, and the body shop bill of $250, and the reconditioning bill of $175 in pending status. Just because we attach the repair orders to the in-stock pre-owned vehicle does not mean we have collected the money. We never truly see profit on the service and reconditioning work on the dealerships vehicle until a customer purchases it. The dealership had an excellent service department that did a great job of retaining customers who purchased a maintenance program even though the brand of vehicle was not the same as the dealership sold.

Now that we looked at all the aspects of the deal, in all the profit centers that were paid when the vehicle was delivered, how does that $900 deal look now? This kind of thinking could change the way the used car manager prices his inventory. If the dealership market has fifty same like models in it, and he has a full understanding of a deal, why not be the best price on the Internet and feed all of your departments?

Understanding the deal can also be taught to service departments. In the same dealership, we had a free maintenance program that the customer got from the manufacturer. Customers would come in for their free oil change, and they would be out of warranty either by a few weeks or a few hundred miles and be charged for the service. For a $35 cost to the dealership, we left a poor taste in the customer's mouth.

A week later, the owner wanted to send out service mailers to anyone who hadn't visited the service department in over a year. On top of that, the mail company told us we would never get them back unless we offered at least a $50 gift certificate. So let's look at it: $3,500 in direct mail plus a $50 giveaway for each customer. Sounds like the $35 giveaway was a deal to retain a service customer!

The Deal and Your Sales Staff

Your managers obviously have to understand how to maximize profits from every deal, preferably across all your departments. It's also just as important for your sales staff to be on the same page. The three-car system depends on a consistent approach, indifference selling, never pushing the deal, and getting all the information up front to assist the customer in finding the right vehicle.

So let's talk about your sales team and the whole deal. If this process is going to be successful, then we need them to not only understand the process but why we take some deals and pass on others. What if you ask your salespeople why they pass on a $1,200 loser on one deal but take a $1,400 loser the same day on the same car. Same manager, same salesperson, same stock number?

Run a test in your showroom to see what your salespeople think! I would do this as a one-on-one with each salesperson. Ask each to give you the top five reasons we would pass on a deal, then ask him or her to give you the top five reasons we take a deal. The first thing you will find is that your sales team will have a hard time coming up with five reasons of why in either direction. After they give all their answers, have them list these in order of importance.

You will find out very soon that the first answer on both sides is gross profit, and then they will be all over the place from there. You will also find some answers that make no sense at all, but that more than a few of your sales staff share the same opinion.

Here are some answers from my sales staff that make no sense. I had a salesperson tell me that we sometimes pass on deals because we already hit our sales objective for the month. He said, "Once we hit our number, why would we take a deal with little or no profit?" I had another salesperson say, "If a particular color is hot on the market and the customers offer was low, we would pass on that deal!" I guess the fact that the customer had a great trade we could sell and was planning to finance with us made no difference. At any point you will see that like some of your sales managers, they really only have a limited understanding of deal making.

So the million-dollar question is how do I get my sales staff to understand all parts of the deal? This may or may not change the way you pay your salespeople, but sometimes it's a good place to start. I find that a well-rounded pay plan that hits all parts of the profit center of a deal makes the dealer and salesperson very happy. The pay plan of your sales staff is important to retaining them. The sales staff in the auto industry has always had very high employee turnover. I have seen numbers in some large dealer groups that actually track their employee retention. The numbers seem to be somewhere around 45 percent on the low side and as high as 80 percent.

I always asked the same question of all dealership upper management when it comes to retention. We seem to lose very few employees in the service and parts departments, so why do we lose so many out front in sales? There are many reasons for this. Sometimes the hiring process lacks a real process. We seem to be so desperate for sales staff that we hire almost everyone who applies. Some of it is the long hours and working on a commission pay plan.

But I think the biggest factor is the lack of sales training. Think about how hard it is for new salesperson in the showroom to try to learn the sales process. The new salesperson watches the veteran salespeople work deals with the management staff as part of the training. He or she watches each salesperson work deals differently and different managers work deals with different sales approaches. Whose plan should they follow? Which one is right? How do we compensate the sales staff for training?

I'm not asking you to change the way you pay your sales staff. My selling system works on any traditional compensation sales plan. I'm just saying, once you train your staff on truly understanding a deal, it's fun watching them work their pay plan to build gross for the dealership.

After asking salespeople why you take one deal and pass on another, group the sales team together with the management staff. Let the team brainstorm on how to enhance profitability across an entire deal. This does two things. It reinforces the three-car system that we already have been training them on and why the quick sheet, trade sheet, and VIP sheet are so important. It gives them an understanding of how to take a customer who walks in with a $1,500 loser ad car for the deal across town and know how to search for the profit in the deal.

A Deal-Making Scenario

Customer 1: A customer walks into the dealership with an ad that is a $1,400 loser on an in-stock vehicle. He has a trade that you could retail and would like to take advantage of the 1.9 percent rate that the manufacturer is offering. The dealer across town also has the car in stock that the customer would take. The customer didn't buy his last car from you, but he has been to your service department a few times over the last couple of years. He purchased a maintenance plan from the selling dealer that has now expired, so he can now use your dealership for maintenance.

Customer 2: A customer walks into the dealership wanting the same stock number vehicle, but the offer to drive home today is only a $950 loser and he or she has checkbook in hand. It's a clean deal—no trade, no bank financing. He or she lives and works about fifty miles away, but that person is at your dealership because the local dealership in his or her town doesn't have the right color in stock.

Now, if you could only take one deal, which one would you take and why? Ask your sales staff and management team when you've gotten them all together for a session on the whole deal. The process of letting them work through the "why or why not" is very important. Have an open discussion with your sales staff with a different scenario. Using an actual example is terrific for training. All you want to do at this point is mediate the discussion between salespeople and management staff so that you can draw a conclusion on which example would be best.

Of course, there are fifty other scenarios that we could've done in order to move the customer into a different vehicle. This training is an attempt to give salespeople an understanding of how to find the gross in the deal. It shows them how to find the profit in the deal today and where the profit will come from down the road. If your meeting had a successful outcome, then the class would have taken the $1,400 loser with the first customer versus the $950 loser from the second customer. The example for the first customer had a better chance of making money even though it started off losing $450 more than example two. With direction from the facilitator, your sales team should come up with the following reasons.

1. On deal number one, the customer wanted to take advantage of the 1.9 percent so we know that financing remains in-house. The average finance turn was about $850, versus $300 on a cash deal.

2. We all know that the customer purchased a maintenance plan from the last dealership. They even brought the vehicle back to the dealership for its maintenance even though it was out of the way. We also know that he or she started bringing that vehicle back to us because it was much closer, and we are the hometown dealer.

3. We also know that the customer has a trade that we can retail. We figured out that our average gross was $2,500 on a trade vehicle that we would retail, versus $1,600 on a rental purchase that we would retail. The $450 difference between the deals is really flipped the other way. In fact, example one was a whopping $2,900 better than the deal two once the trade was sold. We should also add in profit of retaining a customer in the service department over the next five or six years.

The scenario in example one was a basic example of how to find the profit in a deal. I find that as my sales staff increases their ability to sort out profit centers in the deal, it gives a mature understanding of why the Quick sheet and VIP are so important. As their abilities increase, it's also important to move forward to different types of examples to further their education and profit finding. I also find that the management team greatly benefits from this exercise.

CHAPTER 7

CUSTOMER OPTIONS

Giving customers options is a lynchpin of the three-car system. In traditional sales processes, management encourages salespeople to "land" the customer on a single vehicle, and then push the deal hard. That's one reason why many potential customers become annoyed and leave, never to return.

With the three-car system, the process is nonconfrontational with the indifference style of selling. Sales staff and management know how important the whole deal is, not just their own piece of it. And options make it all go! In short, we get the information needed to assist the customer, and we show him or her more than one vehicle.

In previous chapters, I brought you through multiple examples of how we can find ourselves on the wrong vehicle with the wrong payment in the wrong terms very quickly. I brought you through the thought process of indifference selling and how important it is to offer options instead of a one-size-fits-all deal. Consistency in the approach is vital, and that approach revolves around showing customers more than one vehicle. As I said, it's all about options!

A sales process must be easy and seamless for the customer. Many times I see a sales process that slows down the sale and never really answers any of the customer's questions. Unfortunately, this same sales process gives the salespeople even less information and makes them unable to move freely between the selling steps, leaving an awkward selling process for both sales team and customers. These kind of systems look great on paper, but the only people who seem to like it are the upper management who really never have to use it.

A Dealer Scenario

A customer with a strong A-type personality walks up to the desk and demands to know what the rate, trade value, discount, rebates, and selling price is from the manager who's behind the sales desk. Instead of trying to land the customer on a car, the manager uses indifference selling to put the customer at ease. Within thirty seconds, the customer gets the desired information.

Why do some traditional selling systems avoid giving this information to the customer up front? If the systems we teach our salespeople and management team are so great, why didn't the manager use it with the customer who walked up to the sales desk? There is no system designed to handle 100 percent of your walk-in traffic perfectly 100 percent of the time. But a system that's not seamless for the customer and sales team will absolutely destroy more deals than it will ever make.

Creating a system that gets the information we need and guides the sales process through showing several vehicles requires a new way of doing things. You and your team have to be willing to present multiple examples of down payments, monthly payments, interest rates, and multiple terms on multiple vehicles.

In previous chapters, we discussed how important the Quick sheet or quick interview sheet was in picking out the proper vehicle together with the customer. We talked about having a process that was easy for the customer and easy for the salesperson to get some information from the customer within five to seven minutes. We also talked about having a system that could be started at any point of the process, and the salesperson could move between the steps seamlessly without any hesitation.

But there's another piece of the puzzle that brings everything together. I call it the Three-Car System Work Sheet. We need all the information with rates, terms, cash down, trade, and discounts on the work sheet for multiple vehicles. I said from the beginning it would seem like a lot more work for your sales desk at first, but if the work sheet is prepared at the outset, the sales desk avoids having the salesperson continuing to get up from the customer and wait in front of the sales desk to ask questions or change terms.

I find when the salesperson is coming to the desk, it's for one of two things at this point: she has an offer, or she needs a new face in the deal. The best part is that with the manager coming over, she doesn't have to go back and forth getting more figures because they're already in the work sheet. It's just a matter of using different selling and working the comparisons through multiple cars to cultivate a deal.

Let me ask you a question. Does your selling system require the salesperson to come up to the desk every time the customer needs to change the terms or compare rebates versus the interest rates? What is the customer thinking every time the salesperson goes back to the desk? Doesn't sound customer friendly to me!

It's important for the salesperson to have all the answers in front of him. This is where he can now take advantage of indifference selling. Instead of challenging the customer into making an offer unusually low, we now have the advantage of focusing in on what's important to the customer.

Let's walk through the flow of the multi-vehicle work sheet so we can get an understanding of how a salesperson moves through payments, terms, cash down, rates, and a trade. To have a complete understanding, we have to agree that everything is negotiable in a deal. We also have to agree that we need to give the salesperson a way out of the best price on the first set of figures that come from the desk.

How many times do our customers ask us for the best price up front and tell us they don't want to negotiate? And what happens to the salesperson when he delivers the so-called best price to the customer and that customer says, "Great, give me your card and I will get back to you tomorrow"? And then what happens? The salesperson starts dropping the price $500 at a time, trying to cultivate an offer from the customer. The customer looks at the salesperson and says, "I thought you said that was your best price?"

So how's the relationship going now? How's the trust factor? The customer no longer trusts the salesperson. The process was flawed from the very beginning. As you have seen, there are many ways for dealerships to lose money, and this is one of the most common.

Could there be a better way to give a good price but not a best price to the customer without us falling into the common trap? The answer is yes, you can deliver a price to a customer and tell him or her it's a great price, but it's not your best price. With indifference selling, we will lead customers into negotiation by telling them it's an "okay" deal; it's not the dealership's best price.

How can we deliver a price up front to customers and tell them this is not the best price? Believe it or not, customers begin to trust us right away when we're up front and say the price isn't the best in the house, and then engage them in conversation.

- Salesperson: Okay, Joe, I've got all the figures for a couple of vehicles in your price range, plus a bunch of options.

The salesperson hands Joe the work sheet with all of his figures and the written terms. On the top of the page it says "Okay deal."

- Salesperson: Do you know what an "okay" deal is?
- Customer: Yes, I actually do!
- Salesperson: Great, then you know that an "okay deal" is a great deal but not our best deal. You can shop an "okay deal" around to ten other dealers and this deal will beat the other dealerships eight out of ten times. The other two times, a dealer will match our price or beat us by a few hundred to prove a point. If you want the best price, it usually means you like an in-stock vehicle and you're willing to do all the paperwork and take delivery today.

    I didn't want to be too forward, so I just got you our everyday low price that we shop against our competitors constantly. We didn't just look at price as the sole part of a good deal. We weigh in some of the other factors that consumers sometimes forget about. Like on "how" and "who" we have prepared new and used cars. We hand-prepare vehicles with certified technicians instead of an hourly lot person ripping off the plastic on the hood and protective shipping covers on the wheels and saying, "This one's done." We feel that the difference between a lemon and a well-running machine is in the fine-tuning and things we catch before the consumer takes it home.

When it comes to reconditioning vehicles, I have seen other dealers send them through their car wash, and when it comes out the other side, they hand the keys to the customer and say, "Here you go; this one's done!" We feel that if you treat a customer the right way, you will end up taking that car back in trade. Sure it's new paint so the consumer will never know that we put a coat of expensive of wax on it by hand. The dealership has an in-house saying: "If you're going to do something, then do it the best way you can possibly do it!"

Obviously, the above script is rather long. It doesn't allow the customer to interact and ask questions, but its content is the important thing. Notice how we position the dealership as one with honesty and integrity at the top of the list? We give the customer options in vehicles, interest rates, and terms. But we don't sell on price, and we don't push the deal.

If the customer says he or she doesn't know what an "okay deal" is, then it's easy enough to explain using the above script to present the main talking points. This now allows the salesperson to work the boxes on the work sheet.

It also allows the salesperson to get a new commitment without pressuring the customer into making ridiculous offers that make no sense. It shows the consumer that there are other things to consider than just price alone. It also allows us a softer T.O. from the management staff by getting them an everyday low price to pay for it today and take delivery today.

So now that your salesperson has established the "okay deal," he can move forward and present figures to the customer. Remember, everything you showed the customer out in the lot was based on the current monthly payment, cash down, payoff, and credit score you got off the Quick sheet in the initial interview process. As long as we did a great job with the walk around and demo ride, we should be able to put a deal together.

The philosophy behind having multiple vehicles and terms on one sheet is that it allows the customer to choose between options, payments, and cash down. It's giving the customer lots of information, with lots of different scenarios to choose from. It's just as important for the customer to rule out part of the deal or a particular vehicle as it is for him or her to choose one. The salesperson will flow through the examples on the sheet looking for yeses and nos.

On the multi-vehicle work sheet, you find independent boxes showing all specifics of the deal like rate, cash down, actual cash value of the trade, payoff, and amount financed. These boxes will be very important as the salesperson walks the customer through the terms. The boxes will also help the salesperson identify the hang-ups or what the problems in the deal could be.

For an example, using a traditional work sheet the salesperson would have limited terms. I can't tell you how many times I walked into a dealership and went up to the sales desk and watched a manager write "eighty-four-month payments with no cash down" on a work sheet and give it to a salesperson to present to a customer. And by the way, besides that eighty-four-month term and payment, the manager had written down $21,500 plus trade, tax, and title.

Okay, let's role-play a little! In three seconds, the salesperson gives the customer the terms and price that the manager put on the work sheet. The customer asks what his car is worth. The salesperson gets up and goes to the desk and returns with an answer for the customer. Then the customer says that if that's all he is getting for his trade, what's his discount? The salesperson goes back to the desk, and this could go on and on.

Even worse, I have seen the salesperson get embarrassed and guess at things like rate and rebates just to avoid the sales desk again. The salesperson having all the informational components of each vehicle on the work sheet stops him or her from leaving the customer, and it stops the customer from losing trust in the process. Remember, the process needs to be easy for the customer and easy for the sales associate if it's going to work.

So now the salesperson is giving the customer the terms and options on each vehicle with one continuous flow. If the customer says it sounds good, but he has to take it home and think about it, the salesperson says (with indifference style selling), "No problem, I just wanted you to have all the information so you could make a decision based on what's important to you."

At this point we know that the answer is usually cash down, rate, term in, etc. So the salesperson starts working the boxes, looking for a yes in each box. But he continues to move through the boxes, addressing the terms of each box and looking for a commitment in each one. Some managers have asked me, "Why would you talk about rate, trade value, and payoff? Wouldn't it just mess up your deal?" The answer is no. You need to touch on each box for a yes commitment in order to cultivate a legitimate offer.

How many times has a salesperson come to the desk with an offer to buy today if we give the customer an additional $1,000 in the trade? And when they go back to the customer and shake his or her hand, the customer starts getting cold feet and making excuses to leave? Then we send in a closer to find out that it's not only the trade value, it's the term of the loan and the interest rate.

Guess what happens then? We start giving away money all over the place trying to reel the customer back into a today deal. This is why it's so important that the salesperson touches on each aspect of the deal looking for multiple yeses from the customer, constantly moving forward so the salesperson can now achieve a real and binding offer from the customer.

As you can see, it's critical that the salesperson follows each step in the process in order to overcome each obstacle that the customer presents. If you were the salesperson, you would want the ability to answer the basic questions without having to leave the customer. It is imperative that the work sheet shows the customer's rate, cash down, trade allowance, payoff, and multiple payments. This keeps the salesperson in the deal with the ability to find which part of the deal is important to the customer. It will also reveal key areas of resistance.

Let's face it, some customers are all about price, some are all about rate, and others may only care about trade value. So why would we quote payments and terms without showing them the aspects of the deal? Nine out of ten times when I ask managers why they're not comfortable putting that information on the work sheet, they all have about the same answer. They want to only focus the customer on payments and terms so they don't have to defend trade, rate, price, or cash down.

So I asked the sales managers a question. If you're on term and payment—or even worse, just price less trade—how do you know what part of the deal is going to be the hot spot for negotiation? Getting no answer from them, I asked another question. So what if the customer says, "Okay, great; give me a copy of it and I will think about it"? What are they thinking about? Without having all the negotiable points on the work sheet, how does the salesperson know what to talk about other then discounting?

Part of having each box on the work sheet opens the conversation for negotiation. Why negotiate on price if the problem is its trade value?

A Dealer Scenario

Consider this very common occurrence at a sales desk. It's just another reason why full discloser of terms is so important.

- Salesperson: This guy wants to know if we can match a price on this in-stock XYZ.
- Sales manager: Yes, if we have to, but it's a $1,300 loser!
- Salesperson: We do have the exact one that the customer drove at the other dealership, and they said they would buy it right now if we match the price.

- Sales manager: Okay, tell them they have a deal and get the paperwork going and get the car cleaned for delivery.
- Salesperson: Great!

Naturally, the salesperson was thrilled to have made a sale. She went back to the customer and proceeded to write up the deal.

- Customer: Now that we have the price settled, what's your best rate?
- Salesperson: We have a number of finance options available. To best understand which ones are right for you, would you please fill out a quick and easy credit application?
- Customer: Why should I do that? My credit is perfect. I just need to know what your best rate and terms are.

The deal is now in danger of blowing up. Back to the sales desk the salesperson goes to talk out the situation with the manager. Five minutes later, she returns to say the finance manager will be out to review rates with the customer after he fills out the sales and purchase agreement.

- Customer: That's fine, but while I'm waiting I was wondering what my car would be worth if I traded it? I know I said I wasn't trading, but I might as well get a trade value on it while I'm waiting for the finance manager to give me his best rate.

The salesperson fills out an appraisal form with the customer so the used car manager can do his appraisal. The used car manager put his figures down on the appraisal sheet and handed it off to the salesperson to present the figure to the customer. The salesperson presented his appraisal sheet to the customer.

- Customer: Wow! That's an awfully low figure for my trade!

The piecemeal presentation of options has led to a bad situation. The customer is now annoyed. The customer then continues to spout off ten different figures from ten different websites that gave thousands more dollars than the used car manager had given for the trade.

- Customer: If I don't get this from my trade, then I'm walking out of here.

The salesperson hurries back to the sales desk with the bad news. A manager intervenes, but it's too late. The customer leaves and probably won't return.

This is a prime example of why we need to negotiate on all points up front. By having all the terms, rates, trade values, and price up front, the salesperson is able to confirm all points of negotiation by getting commitments in each box. Don't get me wrong, if the customer's only focused on his or her monthly payment, that will be the key point of negotiation for the salesperson. But it is a big mistake if we don't present trade value, rate, and price up front.

Touching on all the key components of the deal allows us to focus on what's important to the customer. But it also eliminates other points, and then the negotiation process that we need to firm up in order to complete the full circle negotiations. I find that some customers need to negotiate on multiple parts of the deal in order for them to make a commitment to take delivery that day. I find that customers are more willing to forgo extreme discounts in some case if we are able to help them on the trade value, cash down, and terms. Kind of, "a little plus a little equals a lot!"

Working the Trade

Part of the three-car system is giving the customer all the information from third-party websites like Carfax, Kelley Blue Book, and Edmunds. It's important to have a trade tool like V-Auto in order for staff to share the whole process with the customer.

In the traditional sell process like some 4 square, or E-Pencil systems, the customer has no idea of how the dealership car lines up with the appraisal value. In fact, most customers arm themselves with the wrong values going into it. They do their own research and come up with values that are so high that we couldn't retail their trade for what they assumed as a fair trade-in value.

Most systems today never talk about value until the customer sees it on the work sheet. From this point forward, it's important to bring the customer through the appraisal process. The process starts when the salesperson gets the info off the customer's car, with the customer if at all possible. It is even better if your pre-owned manager or appraiser can walk out with the salesperson and customers to take a look at the trade. It's great when the appraiser opens the door and scans the VIN bar code of the door with an appraisal tool like V-Auto.

This is a great time for the appraiser to share some info with the customer like how many owners the vehicle had, and if it was in an accident. This is also a great time for your appraiser to ask some questions like, "Why are you trading this? I see there is some damage to the front and rear bumpers. Are you going through your insurance company to fix the damage, or would you like to trade this way? What's your deductible at your insurance company?"

When the salesperson gets back from showing multiple vehicles, but before we present the work sheet, we print off the third-party value sheet like Carfax in order to give the customer an additional opinion. I tend to like Carfax for this because it shows the full trade history on the vehicle. It shows all the service intervals or lack of them.

I sometimes like the salespeople to show some of the other third-party appraisal printouts at the same time so that the customer can see that none of the figures are ever the same from each site. But at the same time, it is important for the salesperson to point out that these appraisals are "not from our dealership appraiser; they are just some outside opinions that I thought you would like to look at."

- Salesperson: In a few minutes I will have all the figures you need in order to make an educated decision. And by the way, if you decide you would like to purchase a car today but are not sure if you can because you would like to try and sell your vehicle on your own before you purchase something, that is no problem. I will give you a figure on your trade that's good for the next thirty days so you can still take advantage of the programs that are available today and have a safeguard to protect you in case your vehicle doesn't sell. I will also share with you the market conditions and selling prices that others are selling similar vehicles for, so you know how to market yours properly.

- Customer: Okay, that's great! I'm still not sure what to do, but let's take a look at the numbers!

CHAPTER 8

ALIGNING DEPARTMENTS

Alignment of your service and parts departments to your sales department can seem like a never-ending task. I can say this: If you are aligned with common goals and possibly joint goals, then you will see your net profit grow every year. The other common thread is that your employee satisfaction, along with your customer satisfaction, will both skyrocket when aligned properly.

I would like to start by giving you some history of a dealership that I was asked to review. The location of the dealership or the brands of automobiles I will leave out. The facts of the story are rather embarrassing for the owners of the dealership and its management team.

Initially I was not asked to review any part of the service department at all. I was told by the owner that the service and parts department was doing a great job, and he wasn't interested in any part of any kind of overview. This statement actually made a lot of sense to me due to the fact the owner of these dealerships came from the parts and service side of the business. It would make sense that this part of the dealership's business would be the most profitable department with limited low-hanging fruit to work on.

So the task given to me by the dealer group was to make the sales department as profitable and smooth-running as the service department. On my first evaluation of the front end, I came upon an angry service customer. The customer wanted to speak to the head of the dealership, so I got involved right away. I guided the customer into a side office off the showroom floor so I could dig into the problem and find out what had gone so wrong.

I'm not going to bore you with the details of what the problem was, but I will say that it could have been handled at the service drive level in about five minutes. I walked to the service drive where the customer's car was still parked, and yes, the customer still had the keys in her hand. Nobody at this point was moving through that drive until that vehicle got moved. Do you think that should have caught the attention of the service manager? Do you think the service writers should have alerted the service manager that there was a problem going on? Do you think they told the service manager that there was a problem and got nowhere?

We'll answer those questions in a few minutes. Let me finish my story for now. The customer wanted to show me the problem with her new vehicle (which she didn't purchase from us) due to an ineffective sales team that had been there for years. I walked into the service drive to see two service writers and one service greeter with their heads down, looking at their computers. I walked over and asked them as a group where the service manager was. They all looked up and said at one time, "He's at lunch, why?"

I guess they missed the car sitting in the service drive, locked with no keys or customer in it. I'm not sure how they missed the customer twenty feet behind me with her arms crossed, breathing fire. Again I directed the next question to all of them. "Is he eating lunch in the building or did he go out for lunch?" The service greeter closest to me turned around and pointed at the door directly behind the service counter. It was a steel door with a large glass window, which revealed someone sitting behind the desk. Anyone in that office would have a great view of the service drive.

Low and behold, I looked through the glass, and there was the service manager sitting at his desk looking down at his computer. So I went to open the door, and it was locked. Then I started knocking at the door. The service manager could hear me and most likely was watching this situation implode, but he refused to respond. Next I grabbed my cell phone and had him paged while I was looking at him three feet away. I watched them page him, then they rang his extension, but he just sat and stared at the ringing phone.

When I looked back at the service writers, one of them shrugged her shoulders and said that he hated being bothered when he was in his office eating his lunch. The funny part was that it was only eleven-fifteen in the morning, so I can only assume he must have been really hungry.

Without getting into too much detail, the customer problem was based on a wrong warranty part that never got ordered. In fact, this was the third time this customer had dropped off her car and the third time she came back to pick it up with the dash light still on. The part never got ordered, so the technician could never install it.

When she asked to speak to the service manager, a service writer picked up the phone to explain the situation to the service manager. The reply that the service manager gave was, "I have no clue what the hell is wrong with that parts department. Tell the customer I'm tied up at this point, and I will call them later on today." When the service advisor suggested that the customer needed to speak to him right now, his reply was, "I can't deal with this right now. Please tell her I'll call later!" That's what led the customer to march into the showroom breathing fire and asking for the person in charge.

I could see I was getting nowhere fast with the service manager, and the customer was not going back in a broken vehicle for the third time. So I put the customer in a loaner car and told her I would get to the bottom of this today. I walked into the parts department to find out about the part not being ordered multiple times. The parts counter person seemed like he wanted to help me get to the bottom of this.

Come to find out, the part was sitting in a bin and had been on all three repair attempts. The problem was never that particular part at all; it was a second accessory that had nothing to do with the dash light problem. When the technician went to the counter and asked if all the parts were there, the parts counter person looked up at him and said no, they were missing one part.

Later on that day, when they interviewed the technician to see why he didn't acknowledge that there were two separate parts for two totally separate installations, he just shrugged his shoulders and said, "I can't stand those guys in the parts department. They never get anything straight." Then he proceeded to tell me about the only thing worse than the parts department was the sales department. Then he continued to tell me how he tells his family and friends to buy their vehicles elsewhere! So much for a well-run fixed operation!

As I started my program in the sales department, I quickly realized that on the surface, the departments seemed like they got along just fine. But given the opportunity, they would have no problem hurting or cheating the other departments even if there was no personal gain. I give you another small sample of this by telling you about the interaction between one service writer, one parts person, and the used car manager.

The used car manager needed a part for a pre-owned vehicle the sales department had just sold that day. The service writer went up to the parts counter and asked him if he had this in stock. The parts person quickly looked it up and said, "Nope, but I can get one by this time tomorrow." The service person asked how much it was. The parts counter person quickly replied that it was about $1,600 for the factory part or he could probably get an aftermarket one for about half. The writer quickly replied back and said to just get the factory one (adding that the used car manager screwed them over all the time).

About five minutes later, the used car manager picked up the ringing phone on his desk. It was the service writer telling him how long it would take to fix the used car and what the cost of the repair was going to be. He said, "Okay, just fix it," but when he hung up the phone, he looked over to the general sales manager and said, "What a rip-off those guys are. I would never have anyone I know ever come here for service."

So the question is, How do I know if my departments are in line with each other, or if they're totally out of sync (as in the above example)? I always start with the frontline employees. I ask them a simple question, "Who do you work for?" Nine out of ten times they give you the boss's name. So I ask a second question, "Who pays every week for you coming here and doing your job?" Again, nine out of ten times they say the dealership's name or the owner's name.

This shows us that if the employee on the front line thinks this way, the staff at the next level must think that way. As I proceed up the line into management, I find the same common answers. You will find even at your highest level, nobody understands that they truly work for the *customer*. So let's start the fix. This is where I bring my highest level management staff together.

Have them draw a triangle on a piece of paper that you place in front of them. You need to write the word *customer* on the bottom of the triangle. For example, let's use the sales department. Ask them who the customer meets first as he or she walks into the showroom. Let's just say for purpose of this example the customer meets the sales greeter, so you would have them write *sales greeter* above the customer name. The next question would be, Who would then help the sales greeter take care of the customer? Then they would write down *salesperson*. Then you would ask them, Who would help the salesperson take care of the customer? Your management team may list the sales manager.

This exercise could go on for bit until you work your way all the way to the top of the triangle. On the top you should see the general manager and above him the owner.

Now turn the paper upside down, showing the owner on the bottom and the customer on the top. Point to the customer and tell them this is who we all work for! This is a good time to explain to them that it's the owner's job to make sure that he gives the general manager all the tools he needs to be sure they will be successful. It's the general manager's job to help the general sales manager so they can help the sales managers. And it's the sales manager's job to make sure he does everything in his power to help the salesperson.

You run through each department, showing them the same connections, employees helping employees, with the common goal of everyone helping each other in order to help the customer. The end game here is to make sure your staff understands that it's not the employee who is asking for something; it's actually the customer asking through that employee. So every time a fellow employee stands in front of you and asks for help, you're really just helping that person help the customer. Once this exercise is done in all departments, you will start to see some alignment.

The next process is to make sure all of your goals are shared by all departments. For instance, have a board in a common place that everyone walks by. On it should be the goals of all the departments. Let me give you just a quick overview of what it should have on it.

Each department should have its monthly goals on it and its day goals. For example, the service shop would have a monthly gross goal of $250,000. Today we are at $155,000 for the month, and to hit our goal of $250,000 we need $31,000 in gross today. It should be something simple and easy for all to understand.

In one of the dealerships where we did an alignment, I bumped into the lot person who cleaned the building and moved cars for the dealership at a supermarket. He was standing in line like me, waiting to check out. I tapped him on the shoulder and asked him how things were going. He said they were great; all departments were on track for a killer month! In fact, service hit its gross of $210,000 with two days left!

I asked him if the sales department was on track to hit their goals. He said yes, they were a little off on new vehicles, but they made up for it in used car volume this month. The next thing was even more amazing than the lot person knowing so much. He told the cashier in the supermarket that if she needed a new car, now was the time because they were only a few short of the goal. As you will see, when the whole team is pulling together, it brings out the best in all of your people.

No matter what brand you sell, no matter what your location is, no matter what your staff and partners will tell you, your dealership will dramatically improve by installing the three-car system. This is not a system that was built and designed just for gross profit. I did not design the system to improve customer satisfaction or employee satisfaction. The funny thing is that it actually does all of those things plus so much more.

I designed the system after selling cars for years and seeing how hard the traditional selling process has been on the customer and sales staff and management team. To this day, I cannot find a selling system that was designed to retain your sales staff and the profitability of your front end, while making it easy for your customer to purchase a product or service. The systems that are used today for the most part are very hard on the sales staff and the customers.

Do you ever wonder why so many of your sales staff want to get promoted? Do you think it's so they can get off the floor every day and not get beaten up by trying to sell to the customers in the traditional way? Do you think they look at a management position as a way to get rid of the day-to-day grind using an antiquated selling system that eventually burns them out?

We all know there is no safe haven in being a sales manager. In fact, the same selling system that burned them out as salespeople, burned them out as managers trying to control the sales process with the salespeople.

Any dealership can have the volume and profitability by just changing their understanding of how a customer wants to purchase something and how the sales staff truly would like to help a customer with that purchase. If you would take a moment to watch your top salesperson work a deal with the desk, I bet it's different from the low-volume sales staff, even if they have been at your dealership for years.

If I was a betting man, I would bet on the fact that the top salesperson has all the variables like ACV on the trade, interest rates, and an idea on what the customer's best price is going to be. I can also say that the management staff will give that person a lot more freedom when it comes to working his or her deal. When I'm talking about freedom, I mean what he shows, if he thinks he has a deal or not with the customer, and what kind of numbers the customer is looking at. That top salesperson most likely doesn't have to come to the desk every thirty seconds in order to obtain info to move the customer forward, because the desk gave him all that information up front.

When I ask the management team why they give so much latitude to that salesperson and not the others, they tell me, "That person is a good salesman, and he knows when he's got something or not." So we arm the top salesperson with facts to keep him in the deal but keep the others in the dark. What kind of training program is that for the sales staff? There is an old saying that always comes back to me: You don't know what you don't know!

I am not referring to your sales staff; I'm referring to your management staff. If they don't have a true understanding of how people want to purchase something, then how would they have any idea of how to arm their salesperson with the right information to move the customer forward in the buying process?

I promise you this, once you and your team embrace this process, you will see staff members grow like never before in front of your eyes. You will also see managers that you thought were only second-tier managers move up to being the top producers in your company. Some of your lead managers that you counted on over the past five or ten years will get their eyes opened wide when they see how much easier it could have been all these years if they had the knowledge of this program back then. It will become apparent how easy it could have been recruiting sales staff and managers into your store with this system.

In fact, we let the three-month-old sales staff member start the training with the new sales staff because the process is always followed the same way by everyone. Every manager, salesperson, and finance manager works the same selling system the same way every time. The same information gets collected regardless of the sales staff's experience in working a deal.

Do you see that when certain sale managers go on vacation or are out sick for a few days, your sales come to a halt? Do you have salespeople that only want to work with certain managers because they like the way those managers work the deal for them? Do some managers gross a lot more than others? This craziness will end when everyone is moving to the beat of the same drum.

I'm not saying all managers have the same skill set. I'm just saying that if the process is always the same, and the sales staff works the deals the same way every time, then you will see success regardless of who sits on the sales desk.

Installing the system is easy and fun. The hard part is having no exception on how it's worked and followed through all the way to the end. Remember the three-car system can be started at any point in its process with a customer, and your staff can still work all the steps in order to achieve the same end result: selling a vehicle and making someone feel good about their decision to purchase it from your store.

I hope I was able to give a better understanding in this book of why we need to change the way we do business in our dealerships today. Change can be hard, and you may not be able to change your entire staff on the benefit of nonconfrontational selling and the three-car system. I will say this: When your culture changes to a highly motivated dealership with everybody heading in the same direction, you'll find it's enjoyable for your team to go to work every day.

So as you read the book, what action will you take next? My hopes are that you go back to your dealership and start turning it around 180 degrees in the right direction.